Part-Time Higher Education

Higher Education Policy Series
Edited by Maurice Kogan

Higher education is now the subject of far reaching and rapid policy change. This series will be of value to those who have to manage that change, as well as to consumers and evaluators of higher education in the UK and elsewhere. It offers information and analysis of new developments in a concise and usable form. It also provides reflective accounts of the impacts of higher education policy. Higher education administrators, governors and policy makers will use it, as well as students and specialists in education policy.

Maurice Kogan is Professor of Government and Social Administration at Brunel University and Joint Director of the Centre for the Evaluation of Public Policy and Practice.

Lifelong Learning
The Politics of the New Learning Government
Geoffrey Elliott
ISBN 1 85302 580 1
Higher Education Policy Series 44

Higher Education and Work
John Brennan, Maurice Kogan and Ulrich Teichler
ISBN 1 85302 537 2
Higher Education Policy Series 23

Crisis and Change in Vocational Education and Training
Managing the Process of Change
Geoffrey Elliott
ISBN 1 85302 393 0

Innovation and Adaptation in European Higher Education
The Changing Conditions of Advanced Teaching and Learning in Europe
Edited by Claudius Gellert
ISBN 1 85302 628 X

Higher Education in a Post-Binary Era
National Reforms and Institutional Responses
David Teather
ISBN 1 85302 425 2
Higher Education Policy 38

Changing Relationships between Higher Education and the State
Mary Henkel and Brenda Little
ISBN 1 85302 644 1 hb
ISBN 1 85302 645 X pb
Higher Education Policy 45

Higher Education Policy Series 47

Part-Time Higher Education
Policy, Practice and Experience

Tom Schuller, David Raffe,
Brenda Morgan-Klein and Ian Clark

Jessica Kingsley Publishers
London and Philadelphia

The right of Tom Schuller, David Raffe, Brenda Morgan-Klein and Ian Clark to be identified as authors of this work has been asserted by them in accordance with the Copyright, Designs and Patents Act 1988.

First published in the United Kingdom in 1999 by
Jessica Kingsley Publishers Ltd
116 Pentonville Road,
London N1 9JB, England
and
325 Chestnut Street,
Philadelphia, PA19106, USA

www.jkp.com

Copyright © 1999 Tom Schuller, David Raffe,
Brenda Morgan-Klein and Ian Clark.

Library of Congress Cataloging in Publication Data

A CIP catalogue record for this book is available from the Library of Congress

British Library Cataloguing in Publication Data

Part-time higher education : policy, practice and experience.
(Higher education policy; 47)
1. Education, Higher - Great Britain 2. Higher education and state - Great Britain
I. Schuller, Tom
378.4'1

ISBN 1 85302 669 7 (pb)

ISBN 1 85302 668 9 (hb)

Printed and Bound in Great Britain by
Athenaeum Press, Gateshead, Tyne and Wear

Contents

List of figures

List of tables

Acknowledgements

We would like to express our thanks to a number of organisations and individuals whose advice and assistance has been invaluable.

First we would like to thank the Scottish Office Education and Industry Department and the Scottish Higher Education Funding Council – the joint sponsors of this research – for their support. We would also like to thank those officials of both organisations who gave freely of their advice and help in relation to the statistical and other aspects of the study, and to Judith Duncan our project manager for support throughout this project.

Second, our thanks go to all the academic and administrative staff, students, employers, families and guidance practitioners who assisted us in the various stages of fieldwork for this research; in particular, those from our four case study institutions. The assurances of confidentiality which we gave to them mean that we cannot name them individually, but we very much appreciate the time they spared us from their busy schedules.

Third, we are most grateful to all the members of the Project Advisory Committee for their helpful and stimulating contributions during the course of the five meetings which were held. In alphabetical order, the members of the Committee were: Stuart Dean, Judith Duncan, Catherine Fairweather, Jim Gallacher, Bernard King (chair), Kenryck Lloyd-Jones, Deirdre MacLeod, Vince Mills, Ian Muir, Pamela Munn, Colin Sinclair, Kish Srinivasan, Tom Tumilty and Mike West.

Fourth, the following individuals gave their help and support to the project, which proved invaluable: Anne-Marie Bostyn and Joanna Highton (Centre for Continuing Education), Karen Brannen, Cathy Howieson, Joanne Lamb and Paula Surridge (Centre for Educational Sociology), Alison Ashby, John Cowan, Averil Gibb and Bram Gieben (Open University in Scotland), Mike Osborne (University of Stirling) and Lindsay Paterson (Moray House Institute of Education).

Finally, we would like to thank Moira Burke, Helen Foster, Carolyn Newton and Marcia Wright from the Centre for Educational Sociology and Gina Temple from the Centre for Continuing Education for their administrative assistance throughout the project.

Parts of Chapter 5 and Chapter 9 appeared, respectively, in the *Journal of Educational Policy (Vol. 12, No. 4)* and the *Journal of Education and Work (Vol. 10, No. 3)*, and we are grateful to the editors for permission to reproduce them here.

Responsibility for the contents of this book, and for any mistakes and errors, is ours alone. The views and judgements expressed in this report are our own and do not necessarily reflect the policies and opinions of the SOEID, SHEFC, or any of the individuals named above.

Tom Schuller, David Raffe, Brenda Morgan-Klein, Ian Clark
March 1998

Chapter 1

Introduction

The rationale for part-time higher education

For most of the post-war period, debates about higher education have been premised on a narrow view of its organisation, purposes and audiences. In this view, the typical or normal student is a recent school leaver, free from restrictive family or employment commitments, studying for a first degree. He or she is able to, and chooses to, study full-time. The fact that this view is usually implicit only makes it more powerful as an influence on debates about higher education. Nevertheless, over the past decade several commentators have argued for an alternative view of higher education in which part-time study plays a much more central role.

There are several interwoven strands in this argument. Perhaps the most important, if the least commonly articulated, is that part-time study has the potential to offer the greatest educational benefit. Tight (1991) makes the very broad claim that 'part-time higher education is in general more valuable than full-time higher education' (p.119). Part-time students in employment can combine study with full-time employment or with substantial family or domestic commitments. This enables them to relate their learning not only to their prior experience but also to their concurrent experience at work or at home. This in turn enhances the quality and relevance of the learning experience and, where appropriate, enables the learning to be applied as it is acquired. Because part-time study is more compatible with other commitments, it is more likely to happen at a point in the life cycle when students have a clearer purpose and stronger motivation for learning than the average full-timer. Study on this basis will, therefore, be more effective as well as more accessible.

Another strand in the argument concerns the contribution of part-time study to lifelong learning. At least at the level of rhetoric, lifelong learning has received strong support in recent public debates. The most powerful impetus behind this derives from economic and technological change, where there is a consensus that this requires regular updating and professional development. (For a critical challenge, see, for example, Keep and Mayhew 1995). But there are broader arguments to do with people's ability to cope with social change, and the need for learning opportunities for all ages in the face of demographic trends (see, for example, Schuller and Bostyn 1992; Coffield 1997). The list of policy documents which refer to the necessity for lifelong learning is endless (for examples, see DfEE 1995; European Commission 1995; Scottish Skills Forum 1996; DfEE 1998a) and the implicit or explicit assumption is that much of this will be part-time.

'Access' has been a key theme in higher education for many years (see, for example, Fulton 1989; MacPherson 1991; Robertson and Hillman 1997). Part-time provision is often seen as potentially making a significant contribution to access and openness in higher education. Scott (1995) argues that recent changes, such as the expansion of higher education and the associated structural changes at the institutional level and in the relationship between institutions and funding bodies, have helped to undermine 'British exceptionalism' in higher education. Included in this is the erosion of traditional boundaries, such as that which marks off full-timers from other students. Part-time provision caters more for mature students; it tends to appeal more to people who may not have had financial support available from their family in their youth. It is, therefore, seen as having the potential to correct the social regressiveness which has characterised British higher education throughout its modern phase.

Another strand of the argument, and another challenge to British exceptionalism in higher education, is the increasing availability of new learning technologies which are changing the face of institutional approaches to the delivery of teaching (see, for example, MacFarlane 1995). Home computers, access to the Internet and the production of a huge range of learning packages mean that the conventional pattern of full-time presence on campus to attend face-to-face teaching is looking increasingly outmoded.

There are also more negative arguments for part-time higher education arising from the growing organisational and financial pressure on full-time provision. As student support continues to decline, students and government alike have objectively an increasing interest in part-time study as a more affordable way to realise their aspirations for higher education. Institutions, coping with the pincer effects of expansion of student numbers and a declining unit of resource, may see part-time provision as a means of making more effective use of resources and of increasing student numbers at marginal cost. In the mid-1990s their choices were further constrained by government decisions to 'consolidate' or 'cap' full-time student numbers in higher education.

Finally, labour market changes suggest that there should be a significant re-balancing in favour of part-time educational provision. The change that is most obviously relevant is the growth in part-time employment, especially amongst women. Whilst many workers choose part-time jobs in order to combine these with childcare responsibilities and are, therefore, not necessarily easily available for study, there are many ways of combining work and other activities, as we discuss in Chapter 3. Added to this is the labour market uncertainty which prompts people to hold on to a job but combine it with studying, either to retain their current position or to improve their chance of getting a new one.

These arguments for part-time education were increasingly articulated during the 1990s. However, as we shall see in Chapter 2, they have not gained sufficient force or momentum to turn the tanker of higher education, even, or perhaps especially, under the fast-changing circumstances of the past decade. In this book we examine the diverse and often marginal role of part-time provision in higher education in the mid-1990s and present evidence from a study of part-time higher education in Scotland.

The policy debates about part-time higher education and the arguments for its expansion raise questions about *demand, provision* and *quality*, which we address in this study. With respect to demand, the essential question is whether the demand for part-time higher education is of a level and quality to sustain the kind of role which the commentators described above have advocated for it. What kinds of students currently enter part-time higher education and what is their motivation for doing so? Who are the main 'customers' for part-time higher education – individual students or their employers? What support do employers give to part-time students and for what reasons? How has participation changed in recent years and what future trends may be anticipated? In what ways might part-time provision be developed to stimulate demand? What is the influence of changes in the organisation of part-time courses and in their entrance arrangements, such as modularisation and opportunities for credit accumulation and transfer?

Second, there are questions about the provision of part-time higher education. What kinds of opportunities are currently available and how does the provision of part-time higher education vary across different types of institutions? What role does part-time higher education play in institutions' policies and plans, and what kind of national system would we see emerging from these plans? How do institutions organise the provision of part-time courses, how is this related to full-time provision and what practical issues are raised in their delivery? Is part-time provision really a practical response to financial constraints or to limits on full-time numbers, as suggested above? Is it equally practicable for all institutions?

Third, there are questions of quality. Are the standards and procedures applied to part-time higher education identical to those applied to full-time higher education? How do part-time higher education students rate the quality of the courses they attend and do they perceive this to be comparable to that of full-time courses? What are the distinctive educational characteristics of part-time study? Is it sensible to aim for comparability or are part-time and full-time study qualitatively different experiences between which no comparison of standards is appropriate?

Overlapping all the other questions, what are the advantages and disadvantages of part-time higher education? To what extent are the benefits of part-time higher education that are claimed by its exponents realised in practice? Are they offset by countervailing disadvantages? How do the perceived advantages and disadvantages vary across the different parties involved: students, institutions, teaching staff, employers, families, friends and others?

The research

We addressed these questions in a research project, *Part-time Higher Education in Scotland*, conducted between November 1994 and February 1997. The Scottish higher education system has several features which distinguish it from the rest of the UK: a separate funding council (SHEFC), established in 1992; the four-year norm for full-time honours courses; a somewhat different tradition of public sector provision in the Central Institutions; and larger and standardised provision at sub-degree level, with a national framework of Higher National Certificates and Diplomas (HNCs and HNDs) awarded by the Scottish Vocational Educational Council (SCOTVEC, part of the Scottish Qualifications Authority since 1997) and a correspondingly large involvement of further education

(FE) colleges in higher education (Paterson 1997; Raffe *et al.* 1997). Nevertheless, when set against higher education systems elsewhere in Europe, the similarities are far more important than the differences. The main policy debates and developments have been the same as, or parallel to, those elsewhere in the UK and although many of the institutional details of our analysis are specific to Scotland, most of the broad themes apply throughout the UK, and sometimes more widely. Basing our study in Scotland offers an opportunity not usually available to researchers on English higher education: the opportunity to study an entire system, for example by interviewing representatives of all 23 higher education institutions in Scotland, while also studying processes at the level of the institution, the course or programme and the student. The role of part-time study within higher education can only be grasped if we can relate the experience of particular institutions or courses to their place in the system as a whole.

We set out with three general objectives:

- to review current patterns of participation and provision of part-time higher education, to analyse recent trends and to assess the place of part-time higher education in the policies of higher education institutions and further education colleges
- to determine the advantages and disadvantages of part-time higher education for the different parties involved
- to explore factors influencing students' (or their employers') decisions on participation.

These objectives were based on a specification drawn up by the Scottish Office Education and Industry Department (SOEID) and SHEFC, who funded the project. By the standards of government-funded projects, the objectives were impressively broad and we had substantial discretion to interpret in the way we felt most appropriate. The objectives were broad in a further sense: they required us to focus on part-time higher education across the whole system, rather than focus on particular institutions, sectors or subjects. The focus was restricted to HNC/D and first-degree provision and thus excluded the important area of part-time postgraduate study, but even in these respects our scope was wider than most earlier studies which have concentrated on first-degree provision (see Chapter 3).

The project's methods of study were correspondingly wide-ranging. We began by reviewing the available evidence on opportunities for part-time higher education and student participation. For this, we reviewed college and university prospectuses, statistics on participation provided by the SOEID and other documents and statistical data provided by the institutions themselves. We conducted interviews with a senior policy maker in each of the 23 HEIs in Scotland (including the Open University (OU)) and in 11 further education colleges. For a different perspective on provision and participation, we also interviewed staff in adult guidance agencies. The largest component of the study comprised detailed case studies of two courses or programmes available to part-time students in each of four Scottish institutions: a new (post-1992) university, a pre-1992 university, a large further education college with a well-established tradition of advanced course provision and a newer college with less experience of advanced provision. We interviewed staff and students from the selected courses and, in some cases, we interviewed employers and family members. We carried out a questionnaire survey of part-time students in the four institutions and in the OU.

All the interviews with policy makers were conducted in 1995 and the case studies were carried out during 1996, with a few supplementary interviews in early 1997. We conducted much of the review of evidence on participation and provision during 1994–95, but we have revised and partially updated our review since then, and most of the guidance interviews were conducted in 1996. We thus collected our data at different times during a period of rapid change in higher education.

We should acknowledge a number of limits to this research. This is not by way of apology or excuse but simply a recognition that any piece of research has to be bounded. The limits are of rather different orders.

We did not investigate postgraduate provision. If we had done, this would have given a very different picture of the distribution of part-time provision between sectors and between the different institutional categories which we identified. It would have given an even stronger sense of the wide range of provision which 'higher education' covers and the forms of employer support. Part-time higher education at undergraduate level is part of a diverse but articulated array of educational provision and most students in our study had taken previous post-school courses. This diverse pattern of provision extends into postgraduate study.

Second, we pay only brief attention to provision designated as continuing education, in either its personal or professional development form. It is likely that the face of part-time provision will change very considerably in the next few years, statistically and in practice, if only because of the accreditation and mainstreaming of much CE. Some of this will involve the recasting of existing provision to form part of undergraduate programmes and some development of new structures and provision. It is too soon to be able to do more than trace out these possibilities and it will be for future research to track their development.

Third, and on a rather different tack, we spoke only to current students and staff members who had some more or less direct involvement with part-time provision. We did not speak to people who had considered studying and decided against it, nor to those who had enrolled but were no longer studying – either because they had completed the course or because they had stopped or dropped out. This has inevitable implications for our comments on the quality of the provision and on the commitment of institutions to part-time provision. A wider sample would have brought other perspectives to the study.

Fourth, our case-study institutions, especially the universities, already had a relatively high level of engagement in part-time provision. This is the nature of case study work. It means that our analysis is of universities and colleges which are towards the forefront of any movement towards part-time provision. On the one hand, therefore, elements of our analysis which appear critical must be interpreted in this context and, on the other hand, the position of part-time higher education in the system as a whole may be substantially less developed than those of our case studies.

Overview of the book

In this book we set our research in the context of recent developments and continuing debates in higher education. We review these developments and debates in Chapter 2. In Chapter 3 we examine the concept of part-time higher education, its external boundaries (especially the blurred boundary between part-time and full-time) and its internal diversity. We introduce this discussion with the analogy of part-time employment. In Chapter 4 we identify recent trends in the provision of part-time higher education and in student participation, and discuss its distribution across sectors. In the next two chapters we turn to the institutional level. Chapter 5 summarises the views of policy makers representing all Scottish higher education institutions and a selection of further education colleges on the costs and benefits of part-time higher education and on their own institutions' policies. Chapter 6 introduces the two colleges and two universities covered by our case studies. After a brief discussion of the methodology of the case studies, it describes the organisation of part-time higher education in the four institutions and in the two courses or programmes studied within each institution, identifying key issues first at the institutional level and then at the course or programme level. Chapter 7 describes the students in our study – those we interviewed as well as those we surveyed – and reports on their educational and social backgrounds and their reasons for becoming part-time students. Chapter 8 examines the student experience of part-time higher education. It reports on the quality of provision as perceived by students and examines how students manage the 'part-timeness' of their study and how they combine study with work or family commitments. Employers can have an important influence on part-time higher education, as sources of support, encouragement or (sometimes) discouragement to students, and through their links with institutions. Chapter 9 examines the employer perspective and employers' relationships with students and employers. Finally, in Chapter 10 we return to some of the general issues raised by the study.

Additional note

In May 1998, two months after this book was completed, the Minister for Education and Industry, Brian Wilson, announced substantial new support for part-time higher education in Scotland. Details of what this means have been circulated by the Scottish Higher Education Funding Council. There are three main components.

Fee waivers

From 1998/99, part-time students who are from low income backgrounds or who are unemployed will be eligible to have their tuition fees waived. They must be following a programme of study that is credit-bearing at higher education level and is intended to lead to a first degree, and they must be a registered job seeker; or eligible for at least one of the key benefits (Income Support, Family Credit or Housing Benefit); or be a member of a family whose net income is below Income Support level.

Part-time course development

Secondly, over the next three academic years at least £1.4 million has been committed to help institutions develop part-time under-graduate provision. Universities have been invited to bid for the coming year, with the amounts for which they are eligible varying according to the commitment they have already made to such provision. Thus Glasgow Caledonian will be rewarded for already having made significant efforts, whilst a university such as Edinburgh is still given an incentive to take some initial steps down the road. Universities are encouraged to review their full-time provision in order to see whether it might be made available in a part-time mode; investigate potential demand from low-income or unemployed students; and build collaboration with other higher education institutions or with further education colleges.

Funded places

Third, to complement and underpin these two initiatives additional funded places will be made available from 1999–2000 onwards so that the hoped-for influx of part-timers can be accommodated.

To us, this initiative is extremely gratifying. Symbolically, it marks a real step towards giving part-timers equal status. Public subsidy to higher education will continue to favour full-timers, including the well-off, but to a lesser extent than before. The weighting towards poorer students is welcome, but it is also good that the scheme is not exclusively focused on them. The encouragement and incentives to institutions also seem well-judged.

So two-and-a-half cheers. There are two interrelated issues on which further steps need to be taken. The first is that the initiative is restricted to higher education institutions, with no explicit link to the higher education work being done in further education colleges. Given the major role played by the further education sector, this imbalance needs to be redressed. Second, the support is formally tied to degree courses, and it will be important to see whether it is made equally available to other forms of higher education qualification of the kind we describe in this book. The minister made it clear that this was only one more step towards a better-balanced, fairer and more flexible system of higher education.

Chapter 2

Getting to Where We Are
Recent Developments and Debates

The post-war decades: the emergence of full-time study as a norm

In this chapter we review the place of part-time provision in higher education since the war and discuss its treatment in policy debates. As in the rest of this book, our analysis focuses on Scotland, but most of the main trends and policy developments have been UK-wide.

Full-time study in higher education has become so much the norm that it is tempting to assume that this always has been the case and that it always will be. As in other areas of social policy, however, it may be the three or four post-war decades that appear unusual to future commentators. Until the Second World War, student support arrangements were very piecemeal, with most students (outside Oxbridge) living at home. By the end of the 1950s, almost all student awards were calculated on a full maintenance basis, but the overall numbers were still very small and a good proportion of the financing was on a loan basis. It was the Robbins Report (1963) which marked a quantum change in the system and set the tone for the rest of the century. Part-time provision barely figured in its deliberations. The Committee's sizeable ambition was to multiply severalfold the number of full-time undergraduates throughout Britain. It succeeded: 'By the early 1980s student numbers in universities had grown to 800,000, the very large majority of whom were middle-class, 18–21 years old, full-time and studying and living at a university away from home.' (Watson and Taylor 1998, p.85). Was a different model possible? It is worth speculating whether British higher education might have taken a different course if the Anderson Committee (1960) on student finance had reported after, rather than just before, Robbins. Maybe the costs of expanding a hugely subsidised system, granting maintenance as well as fees for full-time students only, might have frightened the government into changing the basis on which students were supported. But this was not the case and the essential framework was set or, rather, confirmed. The 1960s were the period of full employment and this was amply reflected in the status of students: predominantly full-time.

In the late 1970s the biggest ever independent review of higher education in the UK was commissioned. The Leverhulme Enquiry ran to ten volumes, covering issues as diverse as Arts and Higher Education, Professionalism and Teaching and Resources in higher education. The context of this exercise now appears historically peculiar in that there was widespread concern at the prospect of absolutely declining demand for higher education, partly for demographic reasons but also because the expectations of demand for highly qualified manpower appeared shakier than before. At least superficially, discussion at this time was about which universities might have to close, rather than how to handle expansion.

However, the Leverhulme Enquiry represented an extensive investigation into future forms of higher education. Unfortunately, its final report (Blackstone and Williams 1983) was published on the same day as the 1983 General Election, somewhat diminishing its overall impact. In addition, it was published in what now appears as extraordinarily poor format and style, making it not easily accessible in a number of respects. However, its analysis was far-reaching. It pressed for greater flexibility in the structure of higher education provision, proposing the establishment of a shorter and broader initial degree with specialised honours degrees and graduate qualifications following from this. But although part-time study figured in the Leverhulme deliberations, it received only marginal attention. The recommended flexibility was for shorter units but still expressed in terms of full-time years of study – two-year initial or foundation degrees followed by one-year additional units up to Masters level. 'Until the 1980s [and even beyond] there was little discussion of how, if at all, part-time students should be financed and supported for their university studies', with the exception of the OU and extra-mural provision by older universities with Responsible Body status (Watson and Taylor 1998, p.86).

In the 1980s much of the debate about higher education was framed by demographic trends: the 'bulge' of school leavers in the 1980s and the predicted sharp decline in their numbers at the end of the decade and into the early 1990s. If the system were expanded to meet the increased demand during the bulge, would it have surplus capacity during the years of demographic decline? It says much for the marginal status of part-time provision that this was not more widely seen as an opportunity to expand part-time provision to cater for those who had left school when higher education was less available.

In these respects the report of the Scottish Tertiary Education Advisory Council (1985) was representative of its time. Much of it was concerned with the institutions, sectoral structure and governance of Scottish higher education. It argued for a transfer of responsibility for the universities from the Department of Education and Science to the Scottish Office – a transfer which would be accomplished as part of the wider institutional changes in 1992. However, it also presented detailed data on trends in the demand for higher education, concluding that 'the number of initial entrants to higher education from traditional sources is likely to decline sharply from the end of the present decade' (p.39). It advocated 'all reasonable steps... to encourage participation in higher education, particularly from those groups where participation is at present low' (p.91) but its analysis and recommendations paid little attention to part-time provision. Its analysis of the demand for higher education was exclusively based on full-time study. Its recommendations for increasing participation said little about mode of study, except for brief references to part-time sub-degree provision in further education and to post-experience vocational education. And nowhere did the report consider the implications of increased part-time provision for institutions or for the organisation and methods of study.

In the event, the fears of a declining school-leaver demand were confounded in a spectacular fashion. The proportion of young people entering full-time higher education rose from 19 per cent in 1985–86 to 46 per cent in 1995–96 in Scotland, and by a similar proportion elsewhere in the UK (Scottish Office 1997, p.11). This increase far outweighed the demographic trend. A mass higher education system was emerging, led by full-time provision for young people. There were several reasons for the expansion. In part, it took place because the policies of institutions and of the government (and Funding Councils) allowed it to. Employers' demand for higher education qualifications increased, partly due to a genuine increase in skill needs (Gallie and White 1993; Green *et al.* 1997) and partly due to a credentialist spiral which raised the qualification threshold for a given job (Robertson and Manacorda 1997). Rising participation and attainments in upper-secondary education, reinforced by the rising proportion of young people from middle-class homes and with better-educated parents, stimulated aspirations and applications to higher education (Burnhill, Garner and McPherson 1988; Raffe 1993). But the biggest surge in demand was from school-leavers seeking full-time places and, although participation rose among adults as well, the total increase in full-time participation was far steeper than in part-time participation. Just over 25,000 part-time students entered undergraduate (first degree and below) study in Scotland in 1985. In 1993 the total was barely higher, at a little below 26,000. It rose substantially more in the two following years, to 35,000, but this increase may be inflated by changes in the statistical procedures used to collect official statistics (Scottish Office 1997, p.9).

We examine trends in part-time participation in further detail in Chapter 4. However, we should note here the importance for part-time provision of the OU, founded in 1969, which is not included in the figures given above. In 1995–96 there were 2400 Scottish entrants to OU courses, up from 1500 ten years earlier. Most of these were studying on first degree courses – as we see in Chapter 4, the OU has continued to provide a majority of the part-time provision at this level.

The 1990s: part-time provision back on the agenda?

At the beginning of the 1990s, one of us was responsible for a review of developments since the first Leverhulme Report (Schuller 1991a). Gareth Williams, one of the original Leverhulme analysts, reflected on what had been achieved since the original study and on the agenda that remained to be completed. He repeated the argument for foundation degrees. Part-time study in association with foundation degrees could go a long way towards the resolution of 'the central dilemma of higher education policy in the 1990s – how to increase participation to the levels of our economic competitors at a cost that is bearable to the taxpayers' (Williams 1991, p.32). The editor made the same case, linking breadth and length with a new temporal structure but with more emphasis on the need to give part-time study a higher profile (Schuller 1991b). The review included a case study by one of the other Leverhulme principals, Tessa Blackstone, of the specialist provider of part-time degrees, Birkbeck College, of which she was then Master (Blackstone 1991). Her account detailed how under-supported the college had been and raised the possibility that the university system would allow this unique institution to go under.

At the same time, research into part-time higher education began to appear, with three books specifically addressing the topic being published in the same year (Tight 1991; Bourner *et al.* 1991, Smith and Saunders 1991). More detailed discussion of the way these authors defined and approached the issue is provided in Chapter 3. Here it is worth simply noting the relative lack of impact which such a cluster of publications had – in spite of a government which continually stressed the need for cost-effectiveness and for closer links between study and work, both features which part-time higher education might reasonably claim.

A higher profile was achieved by a more policy-related project conducted by Sir Christopher Ball under the auspices of the Royal Society of Arts (RSA). A series of papers culminated in a final report, *More Means Different* (Ball 1990), which could not have been more specific in its recommendation of a shift in the balance: 'that the funding bodies and institutions of higher education should co-operate to ensure that the *part-time mode expands at about five times the rate of the full-time mode* so that the numbers of part-time students roughly equals the number of full-time students by the year 2000' (p.60, our italics). We shall see below how far away this target still is.

For the 1990s, Paul Hamlyn succeeded Lord Leverhulme as the foremost patron of educational policy research. His foundation backed a more general inquiry, the National Commission on Education, set up in 1991 following Sir Claus Moser's presidential address to the British Association for the Advancement of Science in the previous year (NCE 1993). The Commission covered all sectors, not just higher education, and one of its key recommendations was for a re-balancing of the education system. Its proposals for strengthening pre-school provision attracted much attention. But lifelong learning was also a major theme and, in pursuit of this, the Commission recommended equitable funding between full-time and part-time students. The expansion of full-time participation had placed student finance firmly on the political agenda and, together with institutional funding, this came to dominate the debate. The Commission's report was influential, not least on the policy preparations of the Labour opposition, but its recommendation on part-time student funding did not have much impact.

Institutional changes

By the middle of the 1990s, four other developments were beginning to transform the terms of the higher education debate: the 1992 re-structuring and other institutional changes at local and sectoral level; the development of 'flexible' arrangements for curriculum and certification; changes in the scope and definition of continuing education; and the growing financial burden of the expansion of full-time provision. Each could potentially, but by no means automatically, raise the profile for part-time study.

In 1992 the institutional map of higher education was re-drawn when public sector higher education, including the Scottish central institutions (CIs) and English polytechnics, were brought alongside the universities into a unified system. For the first time, Scottish universities came under the influence of the Scottish Office, mediated by SHEFC. The five largest CIs became universities.

These changes gave a higher profile to the practice of the former CIs, partly for reasons of status but also because they and the older universities now met in the same policy fora. This practice contained a stronger element of part-time provision and a stronger declared ethos of flexibility and student orientation. The change of status potentially created a vacuum, or at least an updraught, which might have affected the trajectory of further education colleges, encouraging some of them to increase their advanced provision. And since the former CIs had stronger links with local further education colleges, their change in status facilitated the growth of articulation between further education provision and university degrees.

Nevertheless, the 1992 changes re-drew the binary line in higher education rather than abolished it. Especially in Scotland, where a larger proportion of college provision has been for adults or at advanced level, the further education sector accounts for a significant proportion of higher education provision and for a majority of part-time provision. In 1995–96 17 per cent of full-time higher education students and 51 per cent of part-time students were based in further education colleges. The further education contribution appears even more substantial if we exclude postgraduate study, in which the further education role is small, and re-present our figures to reflect further education's faster throughput of students (since its courses are shorter on average). In 1995–96 34 per cent of full-time entrants to undergraduate higher education and 78 per cent of part-time entrants were based in further education colleges. A majority were studying for HNCs, HNDs or other sub-degree qualifications.

The concentration of part-time higher education in further education colleges has undoubtedly contributed to its invisibility and its marginality in debates. The further education sector has always been the Cinderella of the education system; it has been rocked by several policy changes in recent years but most of these have been knock-on effects of attempts to reform other and higher-profile parts of the system. Thus, if the elevation of the CIs raised the profile of part-time higher education by placing its main promoters in the mainstream of higher education, the location of much part-time provision in colleges, and at a lower level of study, may have had a countervailing effect. It may be, with the publication of the Kennedy Report (1997) and other initiatives, that further education is at last beginning to get a more equal share of public recognition, but this is by no means guaranteed. The Kennedy Report struck a chord with many with its eloquent case that the government should recognise the unique contribution that further education can make to widening participation. In this context, participation was not interpreted only in terms of higher education, since further education covers a very wide range of provision. A key Kennedy recommendation was for equity of financial treatment for all learners in the post-16 sector, which, if taken seriously, would give a substantial further shove to the toppling position of the full-time student. One of the most central, and politically salient, issues was the extent to which the Report's recommendations promoted the further education sector's prior claim on resources at the possible expense of the higher education sector. The power of the universities was quickly seen as they moved to counter any such inclination. However, the prominence of the report has at least shifted the terms of the debate and it is no coincidence that the bulk of the additional 500,000 student places to which the government is currently committed are expected to be in the further education sector.

A further institutional change has been the increased emphasis in both higher education and further education sectors on devolved management, echoing wider trends across the public sector (Scott 1995). Responsibility for budgets, personnel and policy has shifted downwards, so that individual institutions, operating within a government-determined framework and within formula-determined budgets, have been required to make policy decisions to a far greater extent than in the past and to account for these decisions. This has meant, in principle at least, more explicit statements of institutional mission and policy and a clearer designation within institutions of responsibility for areas of policy and practice.

Following the Education Act of 1992, further education colleges were removed from local authority control and incorporated as independent institutions. This has allowed them to pursue different markets, or to pursue the same markets but in different ways, without formal reference to local government policy. This freedom has been interpreted in various ways, on two interrelated dimensions. First, there is the extent to which colleges have sought to retain predominantly local links or to move more onto the national stage. Second, there is the extent to which they have sought to change their profile in terms of level of study, notably by moving more into advanced work. The relationship between the two can be complex, with some colleges aiming to combine a strong community role with an increase in their advanced level provision. It is too early to assess the full consequences of incorporation but the general trend has been to a greater diversity of mission and provision among colleges.

Change of the dimensions described above is unlikely to leave the pattern of institutional behaviour undisturbed. Nevertheless, its effect on the pattern of institutional differentiation, within as well as between sectors, is uncertain. Williams and Fry (1994) have described two scenarios for change. In the first scenario institutions develop divergent missions, roles and market niches; their relations are more collaborative than competitive and there is a place for small, specialist institutions as well as larger ones. In the second scenario missions converge: all institutions seek to do all (or most) things, with intensified competition and pressures for expansion. As Williams and Fry (p.3) comment: 'Much of the rhetoric is towards differentiation of institutional function. However the present reality is towards convergence.' This raises the question of whether institutions are converging or diverging in respect of their policy for and provision of part-time higher education.

The growth of flexibility

The second development has been the trend towards greater 'flexibility' in higher education, exemplified by the spread of credit accumulation and transfer arrangements, modularisation and the greater diversity of methods, modes and places of study. As we discuss in the next chapter, the ready linking of such trends with part-time provision and participation is, at best, problematic. Nevertheless, these trends potentially encourage part-time participation by giving credit for past attainments and by making it easier to study at times, places and speeds that suit individuals' circumstances.

In 1994 the Higher Education Quality Council published *Choosing to Change*, whose principal author was David Robertson. This substantial report dealt extensively with credit accumulation and transfer. It made a swathe of recommendations designed to take this forward. Although the report is sparing in its explicit references to part-time provision, much of the analysis of the need for greater flexibility and for modular provision is premised on the assumption that more studying will take place on that basis. This is epitomised by Table 15 (Robertson 1994, p.63), which summarises a number of reports from 1986 onwards, all dealing with higher education policy and advocating a greater measure of part-time provision.

All higher education institutions in Scotland are signatories to the Scottish Credit Accumulation and Transfer (SCOTCAT) framework. The extent to which formal participation in the scheme is reflected in actual institutional practices varies widely across institutions. Nevertheless, progress has been made, if at varying rates, towards a system which is more flexible in that it allows students to build towards a higher education qualification in stages and (to a lesser extent) to do so by combining periods of study at different institutions. The debate about modularisation has been characterised in some quarters by conceptual confusion and organisational uncertainty, compounded by a proposed move to a semester system. Institutions have embraced it with different levels of enthusiasm. But the trend towards greater flexibility through new curriculum structures is undeniable. By the early 1990s, 80 per cent of UK universities had, or were committed to developing, modular arrangements, nearly 85 per cent planned or had a CAT scheme, over 65 per cent planned or had a two semester structure and 70 per cent allowed for credit-based work (Robertson 1994).

The progress towards a flexible national system of provision has been faster and more uniform at sub-degree level. In contrast to England, where HNCs and HNDs may vary widely across institutions, in Scotland they are part of a national framework of provision and quality assurance led by SCOTVEC (since 1997 by the Scottish Qualifications Authority (SQA)). They were unitised at the end of the 1980s and since then most HNCs have articulated with HNDs, which, in turn, often lead on to degree provision within the SCOTCAT framework. This has helped to strengthen links between colleges and higher education institutions. It also explains why most of these links have been established through articulation agreements rather than through franchising and validation arrangements, which are more common south of the border (Gallacher and Sharp 1995). However, the present pattern of further education–higher education links arose during the period of rapid expansion in full-time higher education; the capping of student numbers, together with the consequences of incorporation and other developments in higher education, create a new context: 'the next few years may see further interesting lines of development, in which new forms of partnership between HEIs and further education colleges may become increasingly central' (p.21).

Further impetus towards flexibility is provided by the potential of new technology to support distance and open learning, and to blur the distinction between them and regular provision. Formerly, the OU had the main role in this sphere. It has occupied a curious position in British higher education, venerated but marginalised. In the context of part-time higher education it is a major player, since its considerable numbers of students are all, by definition, part-time. The OU is now being joined as a purveyor of open and distance higher education by a number of other institutions.

The scope and definition of continuing education

The third development was the change in the position of continuing education within the universities. In many of the older universities, if part-time higher education existed at all, it was largely at post-graduate level or through its extra-mural or continuing education provision, open to members of the public and almost wholly uncertificated. Over the past two decades this form of provision has been increasingly accompanied by professional development courses, which were generally part-time. Continuing education, and, especially, continuing professional development, has tended to assume a higher profile within university missions, but with varying emphases.

For the newer universities, continuing education did not exist as a discrete activity, or if it did, it was only in the form of continuing professional development. Viewed from a different angle, however, much more of their provision is geared to enabling adults to continue their education than is the case with the older institutions. The vocabulary of modularity, flexibility and part-time provision is far more current in the post-1992 universities.

For the older universities, traditional extra-mural provision was affected by changes in the funding system in the mid-1990s. Instead of a separate earmarked grant, their financial support was increasingly integrated into the mainstream budget of the institution. This was accompanied by pressure from the funding councils to convert much of their provision into credit-bearing format so that students could accumulate credit from these part-time courses. In some cases, this meant the *de facto* development of part-time degree programmes as institutions recognised the credit gained as counting towards a degree. However, there are numerous uncertainties about the actual effects of this shift, notably in the proportions of students registered for credit who intend to complete even one course, let alone a full degree programme.

The rising public costs of the full-time model

The final development was the growing public expenditure burden of the growth of full-time higher education. There was a growing pressure to contain and, if possible, to reduce this burden while simultaneously avoiding the loss in quality which might accompany any further reductions in the unit of resource. This pressure has had at least three consequences.

The first was the decision of the government in 1994–95 to 'cap' or 'consolidate' full-time student numbers, using the funding mechanism to penalise institutions which increased recruitment. At first, this policy applied only to the universities. However, there had also been a rapid expansion in full-time advanced provision in colleges which, if maintained, would undermine any policy for consolidation aimed only at HEIs. It would also carry a threat of mission drift, diverting colleges not only from their non-advanced provision but also from their role as providers of part-time opportunities, linked to their more local mission. In December 1994 the government indicated that colleges would no longer be funded for a continued increase in full-time advanced provision. It specifically exempted part-time provision from this cap.

The second consequence was the progressive decline in the value of the maintenance grant for full-time students and the shift in the balance of student support towards loans. As a result, an increasing number of full-time students spend more of their time working in order to support themselves. In four institutions surveyed by the National Union of Students (Scotland), between 47 per cent and 74 per cent of full-time students were employed during term time and many were employed for more than 16 hours per week. The Scottish School Leavers Survey, which contacts direct entrants from school during their first year of study, records an increase in the proportion with part-time jobs from 31 per cent in 1993 to 43 per cent just two years later (Lynn 1996). There is increasing attention in the literature to the way in which students, particularly mature students, structure their time (Edwards 1993) and the issue of juggling time between study and other activities, including paid employment, appears increasingly to apply to both full-time and part-time students (Blaxter and Tight 1994). The prevalence of term-time employment has been recognised by many institutions which timetable courses to accommodate students' typical working hours. The hours and patterns of study of many full-time students are now barely distinguishable from those of many part-timers.

However, the possibility of more drastic measures, including the charging of tuition fees for full-time students, increasingly came onto the agenda and, with it, the fear that the demand for full-time study might be jeopardised. This was part of the agenda for the National Committee of Inquiry into Higher Education chaired by Sir Ron Dearing.

Marginality confirmed: the Dearing and Garrick reports

The period before the General Election of 1997 came to be known in higher education circles as 'waiting for Dearing'. In 1996 a committee was set up under the chairmanship of Sir Ron Dearing, who, as chair of the Schools Curriculum and Assessment Authority, had already delivered reports on the problems of the National Curriculum and on qualifications for 16–19-year-olds in England, Wales and Northern Ireland. He had demonstrated an ability to achieve consensus in unlikely areas. The establishment of his committee received bipartisan support, with the understanding that no major policy decisions would be made before it reported. This removed the obligation for either of the main parties to make clear commitments on higher education policy before the election. All parties, nevertheless, committed themselves to further expansion. In addition, all the opposition parties were strong in their condemnation of the recently introduced student loan system.

In the summer of 1997 the Dearing Committee, and its Scottish sub-group, chaired by Sir Ron Garrick, duly produced a massive set of reports and appendices totalling 1700 pages (Dearing 1997). A rather febrile debate immediately preceding the publication had focused on student finance and this continued to be the prime political issue, especially since the government instantly announced that it preferred an alternative system to that recommended in the report. Dearing suggested replacing maintenance grants completely with loans but opposed the introduction of fees, whereas the government opted for the introduction of fees, on a means-tested basis but with the retention of some element of maintenance grant and a greatly increased repayment period for loans. What was very striking was the marginal position which part-time provision occupied in the Dearing analysis and the relative weakness of his recommendations in respect of part-time students.

The Scottish report (Garrick 1997) made a number of further recommendations within the broad strategy outlined by Dearing. Some of these have potential implications for part-time study, including the development of a Scottish Qualifications Framework to link SCOTCAT with non-higher education qualifications and proposals to promote access to degree programmes for students in further education colleges. However, the report had little to say about the specifically Scottish dimension of part-time higher education. To understand the strategy for part-time higher education that emerges from the whole collection of reports, we should look to the parent report, that of the Dearing committee itself.

Dearing located higher education in the context of a vision of a learning society, defined as 'a society in which people in all walks of life recognise the need to continue in education and training throughout their working lives and who see learning as enhancing the quality of life throughout all its stages' (para. 1.10). However, the characteristics of higher education in this society, enumerated a few paragraphs later (1.18), make no reference to mode of study beyond the general notion of responsiveness to the needs of students and of clients such as employers and those who commission research. In paragraph 1.20, 'more of the same' is dismissed as 'not an option'. But after the Committee looks in detail at future demand for higher education, its sole recommendation in this chapter reads as follows:

> Recommendation 1. We recommend to the Government that it should have a long-term strategic aim of responding to increased demand for higher education, much of which we expect to be at sub-degree level; and that to this end the cap on full-time under-graduate places should be lifted over the next two to three years and the cap on full-time sub-degree places should be lifted immediately. (para. 6.52)

The path to this recommendation is an interesting one. The support for further growth at HNC and HND level is flagged up in paragraph 6.14, where it is also signalled as the primary reason why Scottish participation rates are higher than in England. However, there is no reference there to the full- or part-time nature of provision. Then, in paragraph 6.36, the analysis of future demand is split into two sections. The first deals with 'demand from young people for full-time higher education' and several pieces of analysis are reported, suggesting, amongst other things, that the output of graduates may, in the short term, be adequate. The second section deals with 'demand from older, part-time and postgraduate students'. The association of young people with the full-time mode is explicit (no questioning here of 'more of the same') and this is followed by a portmanteau category – 'the rest', as it were, for whom it is 'much more difficult to make projections of demand ... because these groups are so diverse'. (The groups, it should be noted, are neither discrete from each other, nor wholly separable from the first category; many postgraduates, for example, are young people in full-time higher education). In this second category it is only the postgraduates who receive any detailed attention. It is suggested that postgraduate demand may increase by 40 per cent over the 20-year period – 'a sizeable percentage but small when compared to total undergraduate numbers' (para. 6.42). The report then moves to its recommendation, which expresses no expectations at all about part-timers. Whether this is because of the difficulty of projecting demand or because postgraduates are only a small proportion of the total and the other members of that category are too difficult to include is not made clear.

To drive home the tepidity of the Dearing attitude to part-time study, we can look back at his analysis of 'higher education today' in Chapter 3. Paragraph 3.6 reports that over half a million of the 1.6 million higher education students in 1996–97 were studying part-time. It notes also that there are estimated to be 'in the region of 200,000 higher education students in further education colleges' but gives no indication of the split between full-time and part-time in respect of these. It also regrets the absence of historical data on short programmes. In paragraph 3.8 part-time study is recognised as being 'of particular interest in a society committed to learning throughout life'. The report then notes, from its Chart 3.4, that 'the overall balance between full-time and part-time study has not changed significantly over time, but students of the Open University now make up a substantial proportion of all part-time students. Within the totals, there has been a marked increase in the proportion of postgraduate students who study part-time'. These highly significant data are simply reported but not examined or discussed. It is time to do so.

Figure 2.1 shows that full-timers, as a proportion of all students, have remained almost constant since Robbins at just under two-thirds of the total. This constancy in itself says something about the claims that we have moved to a more flexible system open to part-timers. Even so, it might be argued, there are 0.5 million part-time students out of a total of 1.6 million – almost one in three. Is this not a reasonable proportion?

In the first place these are headcount figures, which give a substantially misleading impression of the overall balance. Absolute numbers equate a student who attends one night a week for 18 weeks, say, with a student resident on campus throughout the year. It is clearly better also to make some calculation which allows for this – the most obvious being to convert part-timers into full-time equivalents (FTEs), albeit at the risk of further reinforcing the notion of full-time as the norm. However, this is not as straightforward as it might seem. The diversity of part-timers means that there is no single formula for effecting the conversion. This is starkly demonstrated by the fact that HEIs have conventionally used a conversion factor of 0.5 – two part-timers making up one FTE – whereas further education colleges have used 0.1 or 10 part-timers equating to one full-timer. If we use the 0.5 factor, the overall figure drops from one in every three students being part-time to one in every six FTEs; if we split the difference between HEIs and further education colleges and use a conversion factor of 0.3, the 'half a million' drops to 170,000 or 13 per cent of the total.

Second, we need to look at the system with and without the OU. If the OU is excluded, part-timers as a percentage of full-timers dropped from 59 per cent in 1962–63 (when the OU did not yet exist) to 40 per cent in 1995–96. This is in headcount terms; in FTE terms (using 0.3 as the conversion factor) the drop is from 14 per cent to 11 per cent. The OU provides an excellent service for part-timers, as our own study shows (see Chapter 8). But unless one wants to argue that as a matter of policy we simply look to it as the dominant provider, this calculation is significant in showing not just the extent of the full-time domination of the sector as a whole but the fact that that domination has actually increased since Robbins.

Third, we need to separate out part-time postgraduate provision, in order to get a true picture of the main field, since postgraduate students account for a far higher proportion of part-time students. (It is worth noting that the vast majority of postgraduates, whether full-time or part-time, will have come through a full-time first degree route). Dearing's Chart 3.2 shows that for 1996–97, of first degree and other undergraduate students, 78 per cent were full-time on headcount figures. Applying our conversion factor of 0.3, this means that 92 per cent of non-postgraduate student FTEs were full-time.

In short, fewer than one in ten of the non-OU student FTEs at undergraduate level are contributed by part-time students. The final step is to see how these are distributed within the system. We shall do that using Scottish data in Chapter 4, which shows how clearly this small proportion of part-time students is concentrated in non-élite institutions. The UK higher education system is dominated at undergraduate level by full-time provision. More surprisingly, although the absolute number of part-timers has increased with the massive expansion of higher education, they in fact form a smaller proportion of the whole than decades ago. So the notion that the system as a whole has shifted to reflect a wider diversity of individual needs and a much more variegated set of employment patterns looks hard to sustain. Many institutions are wholeheartedly committed to part-time provision but higher education generally has kept it firmly on the margins.

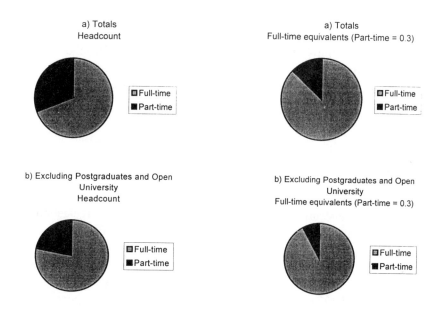

***Figure 2.1: Proportions of students in full- and part-time higher
education (UK, 1996–97)***
Source: from Dearing 1997, Ch.3

It is hard to see that the Dearing recommendation on part-time
students will do much to change this. They were (Recommendation
76):

- from 1998–99 the Government should enable institutions to
  waive tuition fees for part-time students in receipt of
  Jobseeker's Allowance or certain family benefits

- as part of its forthcoming review of the social security system,
  it should review the interaction between entitlement to
  benefits and part-time study with a view to ensuring that

there are no financial disincentives to part-time study by the unemployed or those on low income

- it should extend eligibility for Access Fund payments to part-time students from 1998–99 and additional funding should be made available for this purpose.

As a set of recommendations, these may, if implemented, help many poor students. But they exactly confirm this image of part-time students – as poor relations who need to be helped a little to prevent them from falling into total indigence. It is a striking contrast with the boldness of the RSA recommendation for a five-fold increase in part-time numbers (see p.23).

Lifelong learning

The last phase in our story concerns the actions of the new Labour government elected in 1997. In its first months in office it set in train a wide range of task groups, including, not surprisingly given its election themes, a National Advisory Group on Continuing Education and Lifelong Learning, a group to take forward the notion of a University for Industry and a further group dealing with the idea of lifelong learning accounts. In autumn 1997 the first of these published its first report, *Learning in the 21st Century* (Fryer 1997). This reaffirmed the general role of part-time higher education in a learning society without delivering specific recommendations as to how this should be achieved. The Fryer report was followed by the publication of a Green (consultative) Paper on lifelong learning, accompanied by two other papers containing the government's responses to the Dearing and Kennedy Reports (DfEE 1998 a,b,c).

The response to Kennedy endorsed the report's radical vision and affirms governmental commitment to the further education sector. However, the recommendation on equity in student finance is subsumed into the Comprehensive Spending Review, the results of which are not yet available, so there is no tangible progress there. As for Dearing, the feebleness of his recommendations on part-time provision means that a response is barely required – the paper agrees that the government will review the Jobseekers' Allowance and reports that funding is being made available for the fees of part-time students to be remitted if they lose their job after starting a course.

The Learning Age, as the Green Paper was called, calls for learning to be available when and where individuals need it, at home, in the community and at the workplace. As with the Fryer report, it is in one sense a continuous endorsement of part-time study, although it never explicitly says as much and does not address directly the issue of balance between full-time and part-time study modes. The period immediately preceding its publication was dominated by a debate about the status of the paper, which had been changed from a White Paper to a consultative one only weeks before publication. At the time of writing we can only guess at how constructive the ensuing debate will be. The acid tests will be, on the one hand, the extent to which the government backs its declarations of intent not only with resources but also with the resolve to change the shape and distribution of learning and, on the other hand, how far institutions and other interests respond to the challenges posed by developments such as individual learning accounts and a University for Industry.

Conclusion

Our main theme in this chapter has been the marginal role of part-time provision in undergraduate higher education since the war. It has been marginal in terms of numbers and public visibility. It has been marginal in terms of its location within the system, concentrated at sub-degree level and in the post-1992 universities and the Cinderella sector of further education. Above all, it has been marginal in public debates and in a series of official reports up to and including Dearing and Garrick. Many of the recent and projected changes in higher education affect part-time provision but they have nearly all been driven by the agendas of full-time higher education.

Yet we have also identified changes which have the potential to enhance the profile of part-time provision. We can only speculate on whether this potential will be realised. Will the institutional changes in higher education and further education support effective diversification and, if so, what will be the place of part-time study in this diversified system? Will the greater autonomy granted to institutions encourage more of them to develop and sustain a commitment to part-time provision? Will the various trends towards flexibility of courses and provision encourage part-time provision or are they primarily a means to continue 'more of the same' but at lower cost? Can part-time provision benefit from the current pressures on full-time study and is there the demand from students and employers to sustain an increase in part-time participation?

We do not claim to have the answers to all these questions but we hope that the research reported in this book may enable future speculation on these issues to be a little better informed.

Chapter 3

Defining the Field

Changing concepts of 'part-time': the world of employment

Our main theme in this chapter is the concept of part-time higher education itself: the need to analyse both its external boundaries (and their possible blurring) and its internal variability. We introduce this theme by showing how similar conceptual issues arise in the related concept of part-time employment.

Across Europe there is a growing interest in changing patterns of working time and how these fit with other activities throughout people's lives. In its boldest formulation this is phrased in terms of 'lifetime working hours', a focus which brings simultaneously into the frame the lengths of working days, hours, years and lives, and relates these to holidays, sabbaticals, parental leave and flexible retirement (see, for example, Hoffman and Lapeyre 1998). In principle, economic and technological changes seem to allow for that old Marxian utopia (or perhaps uchronia) of a daily mix of work, physical recreation and social activity – with a good admixture of learning as well. It is true that at the most general level the average working day, week, year and life have all diminished in duration. But how far have working patterns changed to allow the creative kind of mix envisaged by ancient and modern analysts, often from rather different political perspectives?

The answer differs radically for men and women. For men, there has been a concentration of paid work into a shorter and shorter span. On the one hand, entry into paid work has been postponed by law (raising the age at which children are permitted to leave school) and through the operations of the labour market with the decline in jobs for young males, especially those without qualifications. On the other hand, the age of retirement, formal and informal, has dropped, so that over half of UK males over 55 can now be considered to have finished their working lives as far as the formal sector is concerned – though they may remain active contributors to the economic as well as the social life of the country (Young and Schuller 1991). The duration of formal labour market activity – 'employment expectancy', as it might be called – is now maybe three-and-a-half decades, a huge difference from the time when the bulk of the male population entered jobs at 15 and worked until they dropped or until they reached the age of 65. (If it was the latter, the former often followed very soon after.)

For women too, the endpoints of economic activity have moved closer together, but not to the same extent. Their completion of initial education is similarly delayed – even more so now that they are overtaking males in school achievement and finding the route into higher education easier. At the other end, their retirement from paid employment has always been more ragged than for men, even when a pension entitlement was established at 60, almost 60 years ago. Employment expectancy was rarely a matter of permanent paid work, still less of permanent full-time paid work. Childbirth, childcare and social pressures combined to create a far more porous employment structure – though the holes were generally filled by domestic labour, which continued beyond the end of the working day, week, year and life. For women, such concentration as has occurred has been because they have added more hours of paid work to those other duties, which have been only partially reduced by labour-saving devices.

The other key dimension of change has been diversification. In part, this is a function of the overall reduction in working time. When most men worked 12-hour days or more, six days a week, there was not much scope for variation in working patterns. As the working day shrank to a norm of eight hours and the working week to five days, more opportunities opened up for these to be deployed in various permutations. However, it has only been over the last two decades, with the massive influx of female labour into the workforce, that the norms have begun to change. By far the most significant aspect of this has been the growth of part-time jobs. Part-time jobs account for more than half of the net job creation in Europe since the 1980s (Rubery, Smith and Fagan 1996) and the great majority of these jobs are occupied by women. Over four-and-a-half million women in the UK now work part-time, some 20 per cent of the total workforce. Within the European Union the UK is second only to the Netherlands in the proportion of women employed who work part-time, at 44 per cent. In almost every country an increase in part-time employment for women has been a dominant feature of the labour market.

The binary division between full-time and part-time is deeply embedded in our thinking, at several levels. Statistically, as we have already seen, it is commonly used as a simple dichotomy. This, in part, reflects the status of jobs, with far fewer higher level jobs being part-time, and the gendering of employment, with part-time heavily concentrated amongst women. Important contractual characteristics – security of tenure, entitlement to holidays, pensions and other occupational benefits – are closely linked to part-time status, although there has been some change in this recently with the extension of employment rights to part-timers following European Equality Directives (Dickens 1995; O'Reilly and Fagan 1998).

However, the distribution is more a continuum than a dichotomy, with weekly hours of work ranging from 2 to more than 60. More fine-grained terminology is needed to capture this variation. One attempt to provide a much needed more nuanced division comes from a survey of parental employment. Brannen *et al.* (1997) divide both full- and part-time employment into longer and shorter categories. The resulting fourfold categorisation is of 'longer full-time' (over 40 hours a week), 'shorter full-time' (31–40 hours), 'longer part-time' (16–30 hours) and 'shorter part-time' (under 16 hours). As with the number of legs in *Animal Farm*, four may be better than two but it still cannot do full justice to the temporal complexity in the world of work. Hewitt (1996), for example, notes that 'very-short-hours' working – that is, under eight hours per week – has increased since the end of the 1980s and such trends need to be given proper attention.

The variants can be multiplied almost endlessly. Dex and McCulloch (1995) list no less than fourteen types of job that could be called flexible. Brannen *et al.* themselves use a fivefold category: part-time, temporary, self-employed, shiftwork and second jobs. A different typology is presented in the *Employment Gazette* (Dec 1997), reproduced in Table 3.1. This shows that 22 per cent of all employees in 1997 had some kind of flexible working arrangement, using seven other categories.

One of the categories in this table – 'term-time working' – points the way to our primary concern with the intersection between time and education. In this form it refers almost exclusively to parents who take jobs which allow them to look after their children in school holidays (it would be interesting to know if any of the respondents in this category were referring to their own terms rather than those of their children). But, before we move on to this, we need to summarise the arguments in respect of flexibility in order to provide a direct

**Table 3.1 Percentage of employees with a flexible working arrangement,
by type of arrangement (Great Britain, Spring 1997,
not seasonally adjusted)**

	All	Men	Per cent Women
Employees with a flexible work arrangement	22.0	18.0	26.3
Type of flexible arrangement:			
Flexible working hours	10.0	8.8	11.5
Annualised hours contract	4.5	1.5	7.8
Term-time working	4.2	4.3	4.1
Job-sharing	2.1	2.7	1.5
Four-and-a-half day week	0.9	0.2	1.7
Nine-day fortnight	0.8	0.8	0.9
Zero hours contract	0.3	0.5	0.1
Employees without a flexible work arrangement	78.0	82.0	73.7
Employees who gave a valid response (thousands) (=100%)	21,250	11,127	10,124
Base: All employees (thousands)	22,447	11,784	10,663

Column totals add to more than 100% because respondents can give more than one type of flexible arrangement. Percentages are based on those people who gave a valid response to the flexible working questions. Estimates of levels can be obtained by multiplying the percentages by the base.

Source: Labour Market Trends, December 1997

comparison between the issues surrounding flexibility at work and flexibility in educational provision.

For more than a decade flexibility has been something of a 'contested concept' in employee relations. The Panglossian scenario presents the growth in flexibility as a happy congruence of employer and employee interests, with the former benefiting from a more efficient use of labour power and the latter from a supply of jobs which suits their personal circumstances. The pessimistic perspective sees it as epitomising a shift in the balance of power between capital and labour, with management casting aside constraints built up over decades and enjoying more or less unfettered power to deploy workers as and when they wish, at the lowest overall cost. In between is a range of positions which see the current picture as one of continuing negotiation, with some general overlap of interests between management and employees but a myriad of outcomes, depending on the industry, local labour market, national policies and a host of other factors. In short, whether or not you think greater flexibility in worktime patterns is a good thing or not depends on where you are placed in the world of work, what your analysis is of industrial and political prospects, locally and nationally, and what your perception is of people's preferences, actual or potential.

Flexibility is commonly cited as a major reason why Britain has performed better than most European countries in the sheer number of jobs created in recent years. As with the concept generally, this is a disputed area (see, for example, Nickell 1997), but, for under-standable reasons, part-time employment features very prominently in the debate on labour market flexibility. It enables employers to match their workforces more nearly to production systems, whether of goods or services, with part-timers coming in at peak production times. Part-timers generally have fewer rights, for example on job security, which increases the scope for numerical flexibility, though these rights have recently been somewhat strengthened with the passage of new legislation in 1995. It is also argued that because part-timers are less likely to be unionised and are more fragmented as a workforce, they are in a weaker position to assert their case in day-to-day industrial relations. For all the rhetoric concerning equal opportunity, the excitement about the office of the future and the evidence about the work commitment of part-timers, it is still the case that those who work part-time are mostly marginalised in the organisation.

In this section our purpose has been heuristic: to open up and clarify some of the issues in defining and analysing part-time higher education through a discussion of equivalent and related issues in part-time employment. Of course, there are differences between the spheres of education, and employment. In contrast to the reduction of the total length of working lives, there has been an extension of education and fewer people would see a conflict of interest between the providers of education and their students than would see a conflict between those offering and seeking employment. But the summary we have just given nevertheless points to significant parallels between the analysis of part-time employment and that of part-time higher education. Both have to be understood in relation to changes in the total volume of employment or higher education experienced in a lifetime and to changes in their concentration or distribution across the life cycle. Both reflect a diversification of temporal patterns, which is related (among other things) to changes in domestic circumstances and in other spheres of life. As a result, in both cases the conceptual issues are cross-cut by issues of gender differentiation. In both cases the diversification of temporal patterns means not only that 'part-time' is becoming more diverse but also that the boundary between part-time and full-time is itself increasingly blurred. In both cases the concept of 'part-time' is commonly linked to a pervasive but diffuse concept of 'flexibility'. Finally, in both cases the concept of 'part-time' still tends to reflect, and often to reinforce, a marginal status.

Part-time higher education: previous approaches

We now turn our attention to part-time higher education and consider the issues involved in defining it as our field of study – what to count as higher education, the distinction between full- and part-time study and how to deal with its internal diversity. We start by examining the approaches of previous researchers and academic writers on the subject.

Until recently, the fundamental definition of part-time higher education has been any higher education that is not full-time. The reason why this has been so fundamental is the statutory support of full-time study through the payment of fees, which is not available to part-timers. This understanding, however, may now be changing as full-timers pay fees alongside part-timers, even if they are still subsidised to a significantly greater extent. Tight (1991, p.2) described how the statistical categories used have derived from that earlier funding basis and how this may or may not match with the students' own perspective. He observes that 'part-time higher education should not be thought of as a single or homogeneous entity' and we would thoroughly endorse that view. He goes on to sketch out six dimensions along which the field can be mapped (Figure 3.1).

Evening only ↔ Day and evening ↔ Day release

Distance ↔ Mixed provision ↔ Face-to-face

Part-time only ↔ Mixed mode ↔ Full-time option

Modular credits ↔ Intermediate award ↔ Degree only

Open entry ↔ Special entry ↔ Restricted entry

Independent study ↔ Structured options ↔ Fixed curriculum

Figure 3.1: The diversity of part-time higher education
Source: Tight 1991, p.3

Later, in his account of providers and provision, Tight divides provision into four levels: first degree, sub-degree or other advanced, postgraduate and post-experience. In the book he concentrates on first degree provision, on the grounds that this is 'the core of higher education, which has been the subject of most research' (p.53).

Bourner *et al.* (1991) begin their book by pointing to the paucity of research literature on mature students generally, and on part-time students in particular, in public sector higher education. They divide higher education students into four intersecting spheres: full-time and sandwich degree, mature, continuing education and part-time degree. This last category is the smallest sphere – it fits within continuing education, which, in turn, fits within mature students. Both the continuing education and the mature spheres, but not the part-time one, intersect with the full-time sphere.

Bourner and his colleagues note, with reference to trend figures for the 1980s (and, therefore, of course, before the abolition of the binary divide), that 'it may be surprising to some that there is more sub-degree part-time work undertaken in institutions of higher education in the UK than work at first degree level or above. Most of this work is undertaken outside of the universities in the polytechnics and colleges of higher education. It is interesting to observe, however, that part-time sub-degree work is expanding less rapidly than part-time degree and postgraduate work' (p.4). Perhaps because of that, their study concentrated on students on first degree courses. 'We felt that it was better to focus on one of the major segments of part-time provision that is fairly homogeneous, rather than attempt to cover a wider range of provision more superficially.' (p.4).

Gallacher *et al.* (1989) noted that part-time first degree students (excluding the OU) in Scotland had more than doubled over the two years between academic session 1985–86 and session 1987–88, although numbers were still small in 1987–88 at 1746. The OU was the dominant provider and 81 per cent of all part-time first degree students in Scotland were studying with the OU in 1987–88. Gallacher *et al.* identified differences in participation according to sector (University and CIs/Colleges of Education), with universities having a lower proportion of part-time students than might be expected given their share of degree courses. Different educational traditions in these sectors led to different patterns of provision. In the non-university sector a well-established tradition of part-time study, vocational education and catering for the needs of particular occupational groups had resulted in a large number of programmes specifically designed for part-time study. The universities, on the other hand, had provided part-time access to existing (full-time) degrees. Apart from these sectoral differences, Gallacher and his co-authors developed a typology of degrees, including post-qualifying/in-service degrees, initial professional qualifications and general degrees. Initial professional qualifications were more likely to involve attendance on a long day basis reflecting the tradition of day-release in particular professions, half of these courses being in science and technology. By contrast, general degrees were concentrated in arts and social sciences in the university sector and were less likely to include special part-time provision.

Like Tight, Smith and Saunders (1991) opted to concentrate on part-time first degree level on the grounds that it 'has become a key area of policy debate in respect of the proposed expansion of higher education provision, the widening of educational opportunities and the impact of government proposals to modify the mandatory grant system with a system of loans for full-time students' (p.1). They too note the breadth of the spectrum covered by part-time higher education but make no reference to the further education sector's contribution to this. Their research included a Scottish CI and their tabulation of provision therefore split into four categories: universities, polytechnics, colleges of higher education and Scottish public sector. Within this they identify two different models of provision: the freestanding or special part-time version of a degree programme, possibly available in the daytime of day and evening mode, but most likely on an evening only basis; and the full-time degree to which a small number of part-timers are added.

Perhaps the most sophisticated and nuanced categorisation is supplied by Scott (1995, pp.44 ff) in his broad sweep across higher education. He identifies 12 sub-sectors of the British university system, several of which can themselves be further sub-divided. One sub-sector is the Scottish system, which can be split into the ancient, the old and the new. Much later in the book (p.169) Scott explores the fuzziness and permeability of the boundaries which separate institutions and sub-systems, confirming the heterogeneity which has already been referred to and placing it in a dynamic context. But he also extends his analysis to a broader philosophical plane, drawing on a range of social theorists to provide a wider context for the analysis of higher education. Amongst these theorists is Helga Nowotny, who has specialised in the subject of time. She raises issues to do with the intensification of time, manifested in increasing consumption of multiple items (goods or services) quasi-simultaneously, and the weaknesses of mechanical linearity as a way of living or understanding life. Scott applies her thinking to the general social backdrop he paints of modernity (pp.114 ff) but there is the potential for a more specific application of such notions to the specific relationship between time and education and, especially, to the interleaving of education and other activities which are an essential characteristic of part-time higher education.

We can identify two recurring themes in the literature. The first is that the present distinction between full- and part-time study is a product of a particular time and place (and funding system). It is conceptually problematic and may become increasingly blurred if current trends continue. The second theme is the diversity of part-time higher education. It is diverse in terms of its provision, in terms of level, temporal mode of study and sector, including the differences between former CIs and polytechnics and the pre-1992 university sector, and the overwhelming dominance of the OU in providing part-time first degrees. There are also, as Blaxter and Tight (1993) would term it, different 'audiences' for part-time degrees – it is not possible to identify a typical part-time student except in the broadest sense.

Yet there is a paradox in the literature: authors emphasise the diversity of part-time higher education but, partly because of this, they have tended to focus on a small part of the field, with a predominant emphasis on first-degree level study. Arguably, the first degree dominates research and thinking about higher education in Britain to an unhealthy extent. This is changing, as part of the general move towards greater flexibility and, perhaps, especially in the light of Dearing's recommendation to expand sub-degree provision and of the upsurge in postgraduate study. Nevertheless, in the public perception and in most academic analysis, 'higher education' is more closely associated with the first degree, usually the honours degree. Sub-degree work has received little attention, perhaps reflecting the background of most researchers and policy makers in the traditional university sector and their greater familiarity with degree level work.[1]

Defining the field: part-time higher education

In planning our study, we set ourselves to address two questions: 'What counts as higher education?' and 'What counts as part-time?' The first of these questions raised few problems for our respondents. Even the further education colleges, whose provision straddled this boundary, had no difficulty in distinguishing advanced (higher) from non-advanced courses. However, our project initially restricted its field of study to part-time HND and first degree provision, and this posed more problems. In 1987 SCOTVEC HNCs and HNDs began a process of reform and unitisation, which provided an opportunity to articulate them – many HNCs became the first (full-time) year of a programme which could lead to an HND in the second year. Much of the unitised Higher National (HN) provision was also articulated

---

1   In spite of the Harris report, postgraduate study requires far more analysis than it has received in the UK (the position is somewhat different in the US because the postgraduate sector there has been larger for some time). However, it did not fall within the remit of our empirical work.

with degrees through the SCOTCAT scheme. As a result, many HNCs have found themselves with a dual role: they could either provide a stand-alone qualification and/or allow progression to HND and beyond (SCOTVEC 1995). Part-timers are more likely than full-timers to see HNCs as terminal qualifications since it would require a much longer time commitment to progress to an HND, let alone a degree. Twelve credits are needed for an HNC and 30 for an HND, so the minimum step from HNC to HND is 18 credits, considerably more than the initial step to the HNC.

When we interviewed senior managers in colleges they usually referred to their HN provision as a single category. Early in the project it became clear that the distinction between HNC and HND was too fluid to serve as a boundary for the project or for us to ask useful questions based on this distinction. We therefore extended the project to include all HN provision. Since many more HNC than HND students study part-time, mostly in further education, this shifted the balance of our research in the direction of HN provision and of the further education sector.

The boundary between part-time first degree provision and postgraduate or continuing education raised fewer immediate problems of definition, although some of our interviewees in the older universities felt that the imminent 'mainstreaming' of continuing education might erode this boundary in future. However, institutions' policies for part-time provision were often driven by developments in continuing and/or postgraduate education at least as much as by developments in HN and first-degree education, so, in this respect at least, it was hard for us to confine our research to its chosen boundaries.

Our second question concerned the definition of 'part-time' higher education. This was at once straightforward and problematic. We have already noted that part-time higher education is often defined and described in terms of its difference from full-time higher education; at the time that our study was conceived it was still possible to conceive of part-time higher education as higher education that was not funded as full-time provision and for which students were not eligible for mandatory support. But the emphasis on difference as a way of defining part-time higher education masks both the diversity of part-time higher education and the increasing blurring of the boundary between part-time and full-time study.

Writing about part-time study in Norwegian universities, Berg and Kyvik (1992) note three different ways in which the concept 'part-time student' has been operationalised: calculating the number of hours spent in gainful employment, distinguishing between students who used most of their time for studies or other activities and asking the students themselves whether they regarded themselves as part-time or full-time students. When we interviewed senior policy makers in colleges and universities, most were able to distinguish between part-time and full-time higher education at their institution but their distinctions were based on aspects of provision rather than on the behaviour or judgements of students. Different funding arrangements were the most obvious criterion for the distinction. In addition, the structure of part-time degrees in some institutions is different and part-time students may be subject to different regulations – for example CATs and Combined Studies students. Such degrees may be validated and examined separately even where part-time students study the same modules as full-time students on named degrees. Part-time students may be registered separately, particularly where entry/admissions requirements are different for part-time study. Lastly, it was often pointed out that part-time students are eligible for welfare benefits while full-time students are excluded from the benefits system. In this way, the 21-hour rule or the 16-hour rule was an important consideration, particularly for community or further education colleges but, perhaps, most relevant to non-advanced study.

However, for many of our interviewees, especially the institutional policy makers reported in Chapter 5, the concept of 'part-time' provision was closely linked with the concept of flexibility. There are several dimensions of this concept: flexibility as a student 'outcome', curricular flexibility, flexibility of delivery and flexibility of pathways (Raffe 1994a). Flexibility of delivery – where students may follow the same curriculum via different methods of learning or over different time periods – was most frequently mentioned. Many interviewees also referred to curricular flexibility – the capacity to update programmes quickly, adapt them to local needs and circumstances or tailor them for individual students or employers. Flexible pathways mentioned by interviewees included flexible admission and access arrangements, progression routes between further education and higher education, CAT schemes and Combined Studies programmes.

Williams and Fry (1994) expect that 'the spread of course modularisation will blur the distinction between full-time and part-time students and possibly cause it to disappear altogether. This distinction is not known in most European countries.' (p.32). The institutional policy makers whom we interviewed similarly expected the increased flexibility of provision to erode the boundary between full- and part-time higher education. This view was expressed through such comments as:

> Flexibility has been a trademark of further education provision over the last ten years and the modularisation of courses allows students to attend on a morning/evening basis at times that suit them. Students may come and study only one unit or any multiple thereof. Studying an HND like this would, of course, take a long time. Nevertheless, differences between part-time and full-time are breaking down.

> Because of the modular system, whereas students used to go through their career as cohorts, nowadays anyone doing a particular module will be from a variety of degree courses. So there are several different cohorts and so the part-time students are less visible.

> As time goes on I think that we will stop talking about part-time/full-time and stop distinguishing. We will simply talk about students.

Some interviewees went on to suggest that the key issue for our study was not part-time higher education as such but the flexibility of all higher education.

While there appears to be considerable blurring of boundaries, we should add a note of scepticism. As one of us has commented elsewhere, the concept of flexibility 'is wonderfully vague. It is like freedom, peace or democracy: we are all in favour of it, even if we do not agree on what it means.' (Raffe 1994a, p.13). In our research we found no difficulty in making the practical distinction between full- and part-time study, although we certainly found considerable variation in the hours and circumstances of part-time students. Flexibility was mentioned far less often by the staff responsible for delivering the courses in our case studies than by the policy makers we interviewed in the earlier phase of the research. The extent of flexibility in any system is likely to be exaggerated by those involved. In the study described in the previous chapter, Robertson (1994) notes that the existence of what he terms 'phantom arrangements' may exaggerate change. For example, some modular schemes unitise course structures with little improvement in choice, CAT schemes are sometimes adopted as marginal arrangements and new arrangements may regress into conventional academic arrangements or fail to change conventional structures and attitudes.

Mapping the diversity of part-time higher education

Finally, in mapping part-time higher education, we need to take account of its internal diversity. In our research, our main distinction among part-time modes of study is that between day and evening study. However, Malcolm Tight's typology, discussed earlier in this chapter, shows how 'part-time' can mean a variety of different things. It is not only a question of days and weeks, though these are probably the fundamental units. Part-time can refer to part of a day or days – as reflected in day v. evening study – or part of a week – as with day release. But there are units of other duration, calendrical or otherwise – part-term and part-year also – with the attendant problem of overlap with full-time categories.

However, there are further possible categories, often with qualitative implications. One significant category is twilight study (rather a misnomer, given that in the UK and, especially, in Scotland the hours of twilight vary considerably throughout the year and with the diversity of working hours they can no longer be so easily related to the finishing time of a standard day). There are also hints of what should logically, but rather alarmingly, be called dawn study. The growth of shift work, and of rotating shiftwork, means that the vaunted flexibility of part-time study, in the sense that it allows people to combine paid work and study, may be less than it appears. The actual timing of provision is significant for all those whose working hours are abnormal or vary from week to week or month to month.

These kinds of trends are one of the motors behind independent and distant study, of which the OU is such a prominent example. Again, though, this is something of a portmanteau category with huge variety in the demands it places on people's public and private time, and in the extent to which it has a defined temporal structure with deadlines to be met. The advent of the internet and website-based provision means that asynchronous teaching will expand considerably, causing further problems for any accurate measurement.

Level and sector are two key dimensions of variation within part-time higher education and we have already discussed these at some length (pp.24 seq.). Our study, as described above, focuses on part-time provision at HN and first degree levels. The distinction between these two levels is, of course, important. It is, in turn, closely related to another major distinction, between further education and higher education institutions; most further education provision is at HN level whereas most university provision is at degree level or above. Differences within each sector are equally important. There is a huge variation in the level of provision of further education colleges, with some providing virtually all of their courses at advanced level and others offering almost none.

However, the variation among colleges is complex and multi-dimensional and we have found it impossible to devise a small set of categories to express it. We distinguish between 'pre-1992' and 'post-1992' universities, with the latter designating the larger of the former CIs. We identify two further categories of higher education institution: the OU and the smaller higher education institutions (mainly monotechnic institutions, such as the colleges of Education, Art and Textiles) which were too small to be granted university status and had not yet merged with a university. As we see below, these distinctions mirror differences in institutional mission and provision. However, it is open to question whether the pre-1992 universities should not have been further sub-divided into the 'ancient' and 'new', and whether new distinctions are not emerging cross-cutting those described here.

Finally, we would emphasise another, and perhaps the most important, source of variation in part-time higher education. This is the variation among the students themselves – their age and gender, educational and social backgrounds, their motives for study and their reactions to the experience. This variation only imperfectly correlates with the distinctions described above and is a central theme of our study.

Chapter 4

Provision and Participation

Provision of part-time higher education courses

Course numbers

Most research in this field focuses on students and on the extent and nature of their participation. This is reasonable and, indeed, reflects the balance of our own study. Some studies, however, also attempt to map provision by reviewing the numbers and distribution of courses available on a part-time basis, notably those of Tight (1991) and Smith and Saunders (1991). In this section we report briefly on our attempt to assess the volume of provision by counting courses and we supplement this with the means of guidance practitioners, influenced during the case study phase of the research, which shed further light on the extent of provision in those four areas.

We tried to count part-time courses offered in Scotland using institutions' own prospectuses and other publicity material. This proved problematic for a number of reasons. First, increasing flexibility along the dimensions already referred to means that it is difficult to decide what counts as a course. Large programmes may have large numbers of part-time students but not themselves count as a course or count as only one course, thus obscuring their size, significance and diversity. Second, as institutions become more responsive to demand it becomes harder to identify the 'opportunities' to study part-time which may exist. Opportunities may not be advertised and institutions may provide opportunities in response to the demands of employers or to the needs of individual students – for example allowing a full-time student to continue part-time following a change in personal circumstances. Third, as more of students study individual modules and part-time and full-time modes are increasingly integrated it can be difficult to determine what provision is available part-time. Opportunities may not be presented specifically as full- or part-time and may, at least in principle, be available in either mode. However, in some cases this might be little more than a formal opportunity – several institutions indicated that all courses were, in principle, available for part-time study but that timetabling constraints would make this impracticable. Fourth, it is difficult to assess the reliability of the publicity material itself. Some advertised courses might not run – for example if the necessary quorum of students was not reached. Conversely, during interviews at institutions we were often made aware of opportunities to study part-time that were not advertised.

We were able to identify 642 courses advertised by institutions as available in the part-time mode. Of these, 478 (74%) were courses offered in the further education sector. In the following summary, proportions are of *total* courses. Only 17 HNC courses were offered in the part-time mode in the higher education sector. A total of 68 HND courses were advertised, 64 (10% of total courses) in the further education sector and 4 (1%) in the higher education sector. Overall, 76 degree courses were advertised, 72 (11% of total courses) in the higher education sector and 4 (1%) in the further education sector. A further 3 courses classified as 'other HE' were also advertised as available in the part-time mode. These findings are not a simple mirror of student participation and this requires closer analysis. However, the same general concentration at HNC level is immediately apparent and the concentration of HNCs in the further education sector and degrees in the higher education sector is predictable, underlining the relative lack of growth of part-time higher education in the further education sector beyond HNC level.

These 642 courses were also by subject using the 16 Universities Statistical Record subject categories plus a residual one for some professional courses, such as hairdressing, that did not fit elsewhere. There is a fairly even subject spread in the higher education sector. By contrast, there is considerable concentration within the further education sector, where 37 per cent of all part-time courses are in the area of Business and Financial Studies and a further 26 per cent are in Engineering and Technology. The growing flexibility and responsiveness of the system make it impossible to map provision definitively. But these initial findings confirm that the links between part-time study and employment are important and we address this in more detail in Chapter 9.

Guidance and Information

We can supplement this counting exercise with information on provision derived from adult guidance practitioners, who could offer a more 'qualitative' view. We interviewed one guidance practitioner from each of the three regional areas in which our case study institutions were located. We have labelled the three areas to correspond with the case study institutions for comparative purposes. Consequently, area A/C includes college A and university C, area B includes college B and area D includes university D (see Chapter 6 for an account of the case study selection and methodology).

All three areas operate a telephone helpline service for prospective part-time students and in two of the areas the majority of contacts appear to be telephone enquiries – the highest estimate was 15,000 calls per year. Students may be referred to the adult guidance service by local HEIs and further education colleges, training providers, jobcentres, Local Enterprise Companies and companies enquiring about further training opportunities for their employees and other advice agencies. Those who are referred to the careers service may take up face-to-face interviews or be referred to HEIs or further education colleges for more information. In the other area there is an information and training shop accessed by about 30,000 people per year, some of whom have been referred to the shop from a similarly wide range of sources.

We asked what most of the enquiries are about in relation to part-time higher education. In one area most prospective part-time students ask about access and when they can fit into the curriculum. In another callers want to know what courses are available, about entry qualifications and eligibility criteria and where they can get funding support. In the third area the emphasis was split between general types of enquiry such as 'Where can I do a part-time degree?' and 'What subjects are available for part-time study?' and more specific questions on, for example, what part-time routes are available to develop professional knowledge in a particular subject. Funding issues were considered to be intrinsic to all such enquiries.

Interviewees were invited to consider how the balance of enquiries had changed in respect of part-time higher education students over the last three to five years. In area B it was suggested that, due to part-time funding constraints, more people are thinking about returning to education on a full-time basis and that part-time education is often perceived as very much an evening-class scenario. However, the practitioner felt that the guidance service had improved by showing prospective students a range of different progression routes to complement their financial, domestic and work circumstances and by getting across the message that people can work, learn and train at the same time.

Some of these views were supported in area D, where the practitioner thought there was a growing awareness of the option to go part-time – due partly to publicity and promotion, both professionally and by word of mouth, and partly to university D being proactive in promoting its part-time courses and extending the range of its provision. Higher levels of unemployment and redundancy were also thought to be changing the profile of students away from 'middle-class ladies with time on their hands' towards more students from 'lower social classes' – our interviewee stressed that this was very much a generalisation. In area A/C the emphasis was on more interest in part-time higher education shown by callers, more part-time provision by further education colleges and HEIs and the growth of CATs schemes and accreditation of continuing education courses – all of which has led to an increase in the perceived value of qualifications gained through part-time study.

Practitioners were asked whether the provision of opportunities for part-time higher education in their areas was adequate or whether there are gaps in terms of level, subject, location and mode of attendance. Responses varied. In one area the perceived gaps were not so much curricular as in terms of flexibility of access to education and training at times which suited the students. The practitioner felt that training providers for further education and higher education could be more flexible and that there was scope for more people in full-time employment accessing higher education opportunities – currently, unless their employers allow them time off to attend timetabled classes, employees are unable to study part-time. Supported training in the workplace was felt to be another area where improvements could be made.

In area D, due to the development of part-time courses at university D, there were thought to be few subjects unavailable to part-time students, with the exception of science and engineering, but part-time opportunities for daytime study were limited, given that part-timers would have to be infilled into the existing full-time classes which are spread throughout the week. However, university D's Summer Academic Programme affords part-time students an additional option to study during the summer months and enables part-timers to complete their degrees more quickly.

In the third area the practitioner explained that gaps were not always perceived until enquiries were being followed up by guidance advisers. She felt that provision has improved, particularly due to

CATs schemes and the accreditation of continuing education courses, although she had reservations about whether the expansion of part-time higher education was geared to meet the needs of prospective students as much as it was geared to enable institutions to attract 'a different type of client'. Perhaps surprisingly, due to the proliferation of institutions in the area, she identified a number of curricular gaps at both HN and first-degree levels, based on enquiries which had been received. However, she added that whilst some local institutions did offer most of these types of subject, demand often exceeded supply.

We asked about the relative importance to prospective part-time higher education students of prospectuses and other paper resources and information from verbal guidance and support. The varied responses signalled the different approaches adopted by guidance practitioners in each area. One actively encourages visitors to do a lot of their own research by accessing interactive databases and believes this allows the guidance intervention to be much more productive, enabling prospective students to be more committed to assessing their opportunities and preparing more effective action plans through being better informed. Another tended to give verbal guidance in the first instance to prospective students, particularly those who lack confidence, need reassurance and would benefit from being informed about their opportunities. Paper resources were perceived to have limited value as there was a danger of mature returners suffering from information overload when confronted by bulky prospectuses. Prospective students were encouraged to contact someone associated with the delivery of courses at the local HEI, whose staff were said to be very approachable.

One of the characteristics of area A/C was the large number of local institutions from which prospective students could choose and, for this reason, the opposite approach was adopted there. The national databases for further education, higher education and graduate opportunities were not thought to be 'terribly good for Scotland' as they only reflect information which had been provided by institutions, the usefulness of which was variable. The practitioner found it necessary to refer to individual prospectuses in the first instance when dealing with specific telephone enquiries to find out exactly what provision was available. In some cases the prospectus was the only source. More in-depth verbal guidance from advisers was given at the follow-up stage.

Practitioners were asked if they thought there was untapped demand for part-time higher education in their area and, if so, why. All three believed there was untapped demand. In areas B and D this was considered to be predominantly because many people were unaware of the opportunities which were available, had never considered returning to learning and were unlikely to understand what it involved. In area B the practitioner felt that more could be done to tailor provision to meet students' needs and that, for this to be done, the first stage was to identify people's needs. In area A/C, however, the perception was that there was insufficient provision of various courses to meet demand.

Finally, we asked what factors discouraged potential students from entering part-time higher education. All three practitioners put cost at the top of their list. Other potential barriers mentioned were domestic responsibilities and inaccessibility, due either to geographical remoteness from delivery points or to lack of funding, in area B; curricular gaps, timetabling restrictions, travel, the time required, lack of childcare provision and uncertainty that learning could improve employment prospects in area D; and time commitments, inability to manage time, location and mode of attendance in area A/C.

Student participation

The discussion above has already shown that higher education provision is not coterminous with the higher education sector and that this is particularly the case with part-time higher education. That is the rationale for including further education colleges as we have done. Within the higher education sector we need to allocate institutions to different categories in order to give proper shape to the analysis. The most obvious approach is to use the categories which obtain historically, retaining a distinction between the post-1992 former Central Institutions and pre-1992 universities, holding the OU in a separate category of its own and using a residual category for non-university HEIs. Together with further education colleges, this gives us five categories. We considered sub-dividing the further education category into two by separating members of the unofficial Scotland's Polytechnic Colleges grouping – characterised as large, serving a wide hinterland and offering a substantial range of higher education – from the rest. We did not do so because we judged that further education colleges varied along several dimensions and represented a continuum within each dimension, so that a sub-division into two or three categories would be less useful for analytical purposes.

We present data on the participation of part-time students in different sectors and categories of our typology, according to different levels. This gives an overall picture of the distribution of part-time participants. It allows us to gauge the significance of part-time participation from several angles and at different levels. Significance can be judged in terms of numbers of part-timers in an institution, category or sector in relation to the overall total of part-timers, or of these numbers as a proportion of a sector, category or institution's total enrolments. We have done this below in respect of sectors and categories but not in relation to individual institutions.

This section first examines trends in participation for the ten-year period 1983–84 to 1993–94. It then analyses participation in more detail for the year 1993–94, the last year for which comparable and detailed data was available. The following section provides data for more recent years but, as we explain there, it is not strictly comparable.

Trends in participation 1983–84 to 1993–94

The following analysis is based on statistics provided to us by the SOEID for the period 1983–84 to 1993–94. The OU has been excluded from the calculation of general trends and is dealt with separately.

Students

Participation in full-time higher education remained relatively stable during much of the 1980s until 1988, when a period of rapid expansion began. In general, full-time participation expanded much faster than part-time participation. Full-time student numbers nearly doubled from 76,487 in 1983–84 to 132,509 in 1993–94. The increase in full-time higher education students at all levels over the period was 73 per cent. The growth in part-time student numbers was far less dramatic, increasing from 35,575 students in 1983–84 to 47,220 in 1993–94 – an increase in part-time student numbers at all levels of 33 per cent over the ten years, dropping to 19 per cent when postgraduate study is excluded. The growth in part-time student numbers was also less consistent, so that when postgraduate study is excluded, the figures show percentage decreases in four out of the ten years. There were variations in the rates of growth by sector and level.

Full-time student numbers at all levels in HEIs (excluding postgraduate study) rose from 62,958 in 1983–84 to 98,440 in 1993–94 – an increase of 56 per cent. This compared with an increase from 6148 to 20,221 for the same group in further education colleges – an increase of 229 per cent. The highest increases in the further education sector were in the number of full-time HN students, particularly HNCs. HN students accounted for 94 per cent of all full-time higher education students studying in further education colleges in 1993–94. The greatest increase in full-time students in HEIs was at postgraduate level, at 89 per cent over the ten years. This was closely followed by first degree study at 72 per cent where, of course, absolute numbers were much higher at 54,235 in 1983–84 and 93,172 in 1993–94.

Part-time student numbers at all levels in HEIs (excluding postgraduate study) rose from 9436 in 1983–84 to 10,653 in 1993–94 – an increase of 13 per cent compared with an increase of 21 per cent for the same group in further education colleges. Absolute (headcount) numbers of part-time students in further education colleges were much higher at 22,020 in 1983–84 and 26,649 in 1993–94 (excluding postgraduate study). In 1993–94 nearly half (48%) of all part-time higher education students in HEIs were studying at postgraduate level and a further 31 per cent were studying for a first degree. There was a significant increase in part-time study at both these levels in HEIs, at 136 per cent for postgraduate study and 249 per cent for first degree study, but absolute numbers in these groups were small. In the further education sector the most significant growth was in HNC study, where there was a percentage increase of 193 per cent over the ten years. Although there were significant increases in postgraduate study and first degree study in this sector, absolute numbers were very small, making HNC by far the most significant level of study in the part-time mode in the further education sector. Throughout this period the OU in Scotland continued to dominate as a provider of part-time degrees. Student numbers at all levels of study nearly doubled during the period, increasing from 7037 in 1983–84 to 12,232 in 1993–94.

Table 4.1 Percentage changes in higher education entrants in Scotland 1983/4–1993/4

Year	Part-time entrants		Full-time entrants	
	All levels	Excluding postgraduate	All levels	Excluding postgraduate
1983–84	5.3	4.5	2.3	2.0
1984–85	-1.1	-2.0	1.8	2.3
1985–86	11.0	10.1	3.5	1.9
1986–87	0.7	0.4	3.8	2.2
1987–88	0.3	-0.1	1.9	3.7
1988–89	-3.6	-3.9	1.6	1.6
1989–90	3.2	2.0	12.7	12.9
1990–91	-1.6	-2.0	6.9	5.6
1991–92	2.9	1.2	14.8	14.3
1992–93	10.9	10.5	13.3	15.5
1993–94	-3.7	-4.4	10.9	11.8

Source: Scottish Office Education and Industry Department

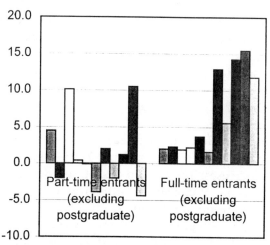

Figure 4.1 Percentage changes in higher education entrants by year 1983/4 to 1993/4

Entrants

An analysis of percentage changes in entrants to higher education over these ten years reveals similar contrasts between trends in full-time and part-time numbers. The greatest percentage increase over the ten years is in full-time entrants – 97 per cent at all levels compared with an increase of 19 per cent for part-time entrants, dropping to 11 per cent when postgraduate study is excluded. Table 4.1 shows that the rate of growth in full-time entrants is slow but steady until 1989–90 when there is a significant increase in the rate of growth, jumping from 1.6 per cent in 1988–89 to 12.7 per cent in 1989–90. For four out of the six years from 1989–90, the percentage increase is in double figures, reaching a high of 14.8 per cent between 1990–91 and 1991–92. By contrast, the rate of growth in part-time entrants has been far from steady. There has been a percentage fall in the number of entrants in five out of the ten years and the rate of growth has been inconsistent, varying from an increase of 10.9 per cent in 1992–93 to a fall of 3.7 per cent in the following academic year. Figure 4.1 shows this graphically.

Analysis of percentage changes in entrants by level and sector reveals a similar pattern of differences to that of student numbers. Particularly noteworthy is the contrast between part-time and full-time entrants in the further education sector, where percentage increases in entrants to advanced courses (excluding postgraduate study) were 12 per cent and 320 per cent respectively over the ten years. The rapid expansion of full-time higher education entrants in the further education sector over the period in absolute and relative terms meant that almost half of the further education sector's higher education entrants in 1993–94 were full-time.

There is no sense from these data that part-time study 'took off' in the period of major higher education expansion. On the contrary, yearly increases in the number of entrants to part-time higher education have been small and decreases in both student numbers and entrants during the ten years up until 1993–94 have been nearly as frequent as increases. There is no clear trend demonstrating that part-time study is increasing significantly overall, particularly in the context of the expansion of full-time study. Moreover, in the case of part-time study, percentage changes from one year to another appear to be a poor predictor of future years. In short, the dramatic increases in full-time entrants and students over these ten years have served to increase the preponderance of full-time over part-time study, in effect further the part-time mode.

Student participation 1993–94

The following tables were derived from data supplied by the SOEID and are for the year 1993–94 with the exception of the OU, where statistics are for the year 1992–93 because this was the last year for which detailed published data were available. However, these figures incorporate a few changes to the 1993–94 data. In the course of our fieldwork we became aware of some inaccuracies in the statistics, particularly when courses offered jointly with another institution, or service courses provided for another institution's students, were recorded as part-time even though their students were studying full-time. In the following tables we have corrected for the two large instances of this of which we became aware. The result, in both cases, is to increase the contrast between further education and higher education sectors in respect of the levels of part-time provision.

Table 4.2 shows that nearly half (46%) of part-time students in Scotland were studying in the further education sector, 18 per cent were studying with the OU, a further 18 per cent with the post-1992 universities and 16 per cent were studying part-time at the pre-1992 universities. Under 2 per cent were studying at 'other HEIs'.

To simplify the following analyses we omit postgraduate study. Table 4.3 shows the percentages of students studying at each level. If postgraduate study is excluded, 56 per cent of all part-time students were studying in the further education sector, 21 per cent were with the OU and 18 per cent were studying at the post-1992 universities. The pre-1992 universities had less than 4 per cent of the total part-time students and 'other HEIs' had less than 2 per cent. (The vast majority of part-time students in the pre-1992 universities were postgraduates). Over half (56%) of all part-time first degree students were studying with the OU. Table 4.4 is based on the same figures as Table 4.3, with the percentages the other way round. Students at each level of study are shown as a percentage of all part-time students (excluding postgraduates) within the sectors. The table casts further light on the continuation of further education as a part-time provider – two-thirds (66%) of part-time further education students were studying for HNC/Ds and most of the remainder were taking 'other HE' courses. Of all part-time higher education students in Scotland (excluding postgraduates), 37 per cent were studying for an HNC, 34 per cent for a first degree, 27 per cent were studying on some other higher education course and only 3 per cent were studying part-time for an HND.

While these data give a clear picture of the distribution of part-time students by level and sector, it is necessary to compare them with a similar analysis for full-time students in order to gain a clear sense of the significance of the part-time mode. Table 4.5 shows numbers of all full-time students for 1993–94 and may be compared with Table 4.2. Table 4.5 shows a fairly predictable pattern of participation. Over half (53%) of all full-time students were studying at a pre-1992 university and the majority (71%) of all full-time higher education students were studying for a first degree.

Table 4.6 shows the percentage of all higher education students who were part-time by level and sector. Apart from the OU (which is omitted since all its students are part-time) the further education sector has the highest proportions of part-time students (56%), followed by the post-1992 universities at 26 per cent. The sectoral differences change if postgraduate study is removed. The changes are minor except in the case of the pre-1992 universities, where the proportion of higher education students studying part-time drops to 3 per cent.

Table 4.2 Part-time student numbers by sector and level 1993–94

Sector	Post-graduate	First degree	HND	HNC	Other HE	Total	%
Post–1992 university	1,751	4,464	454	680	2,816	10,165	18
Pre–1992 university	7,619	1,646	0	0	0	9,265	16
Open University	481	8,655	0	0	1,154	10,290	18
Other HE!s	283	373	0	17	238	911	2
FE colleges	265	445	862	16,283	8,230	26,085	46
Total (no.)	10,399	15,583	1,316	16,980	12,438	56,716	
%	18	28	2	30	22		100

Source: Scottish Office Education and Industry Department

Table 4.3 Educational sector of part-time students by level of study (percentages; excluding postgraduate)

Type	First degree	HND	HNC	Other HE	All levels
Post–1992 university	29	34	4	23	18
Pre–1992 university	11	0	0	0	4
Open university	56	0	0	9	21
Other HEIs	2	0	0	2	1
FE colleges	3	66	96	66	56
Total	101	100	100	100	100

Source: Scottish Office Education and Industry Department

Table 4.4 Level of studies of part-time students by educational sector (percentages) 1993–94

Sector	Post-1992 university	Pre-1992 university	Open university	Other HEIs	FE colleges	All sectors
First degree	53	100	88	59	2	34
HND	5	0	0	0	3	3
HNC	8	0	0	3	63	37
Other HE	33	0	12	38	32	27
Total	99	100	100	100	100	101

Source: Scottish Office Education and Industry Department

Table 4.5 Full-time student numbers by sector and level 1993–94

Sector	Post-graduate	First degree	HND	HNC	Other HE	Total	%
Post–1992 university	2,152	23,165	2,920	139	648	29,024	22
Pre-1992 university	10,010	59,935	0	0	67	70,012	53
Other HEIs	1,565	9,947	524	49	480	12,565	10
FE colleges	121	222	11,053	8,123	823	20,342	15
Total (no.)	13,848	93,269	14,497	8,311	2,018	131,943	
%	10	71	11	6	2		100

Source: Scottish Office Education and Industry Department

Table 4.6 Percentage of all students who are part-time by level and sector 1993–94

Sector	Post-graduate	First degree	HND	HNC	Other HE	All levels
Post-1992 university	45	16	13	83	81	26
Pre-1992 university	43	3	0	0	0	12
Other HEIs	15	4	0	26	33	7
FE colleges	69	67	7	67	91	56

Source: Scottish Office Education and Industry Department

Participation since 1994–95

Although our fieldwork was carried out in 1995–96, our own statistical analysis was carried out on data only covering the period up to 1993–94. As it happens, this marked a significant caesura in statistical collection, which makes it impossible to update our figures straightforwardly. The December 1997 SHEFC Statistical Bulletin explains: '1994–95 was the first session in which HESA (the Higher Education Statistics Agency) collected information, and the coverage of HESA's returns differs from that of the former data collecting bodies. *The figures for 1994–95 and 1995–96 for both full-time and part-time students are not directly comparable with those*

Table 4.7 Total higher education student numbers for academic year 1994–95, undergraduate and postgraduate, by full-time and part-time mode

	All	*Undergraduate*				*Postgraduate*			
	Total	*Total*	*Full-time*	*Part-time*	*% Part-time*	*Total*	*Full-time*	*Part-time*	*% Part-time*
Pre-1992 universities	90,500	67,000	64,300	2,700	4	23,500	11,400	12,100	51
New universities	41,400	37,100	29,100	7,900	21	4,300	2,300	2,000	48
Colleges of Education	7,300	3,600	3,200	300	9	3,700	1,000	2,700	74
Other Institutions	8,400	7,600	7,100	500	7	800	600	200	25
Open university: Scots	14,100	12,200	0	12,200	100	2,000	30	1,900	98
FE Colleges	55,000	54,200	24,100	30,100	56	800	100	600	83
Total	217,000	182,000	128,000	54,000	30	35,000	15,000	20,000	56

Source: from Raab and Johnston (1997)

Part-Time Higher Education

Table 4.8 Students on credit-bearing courses in HEIs 1995–96

A. Numbers of students

	Individual Student Returns							Total
	Postgraduate				Undergraduate and below			
	Full-time and sandwich	Part-time (inc short full-time)	Total	Of which: Research students	Full-time and sandwich	Part-time (inc short full-time)	Total	
Pre-1992 university	11,520	10,683	22,203	6,545	64,805	4,970	69,775	91,978
Post-1992 university	2,733	2,553	5,286	703	29,033	8,011	37,044	42,330
Others	1,337	3,244	4,581	192	9,238	928	10,166	14,747
Total	15,590	16,480	32,070	7,440	103,076	13,909	116,985	149,055

B. Full-time equivalents

	Individual Student Returns							Total
	Postgraduate				Undergraduate and below			
	Full-time and sandwich	Part-time (inc short full-time)	Total	Of which: Research students	Full-time and sandwich	Part-time (inc short full-time)	Total	
Pre-1992 university	9,904	3,997	13,901	5,318	62,950	1,478	64,427	78,329
Post-1992 university	2,521	1,156	3,677	548	27,634	3,371	31,005	34,680
Others	1,224	701	1,925	120	9,085	396	9,483	11,407
Total	13,649	5,854	19,503	5,986	99,669	5,245	104,915	124,416

Source: calculated from SHEFC Statistical Bulletin 3/97, *Higher Education Institutions: Students and Staff 1995–96 for previous years.'* (SHEFC 1997, p.6, italics in original). Nor are 1994–95 and 1995–96 themselves directly comparable since there was a further change (in the so-called Standard Population) between one year and the next. More than that, the changes in the coverage were particularly great in respect of part-time students, so much so in some institutions that it has been impossible for comparable figures for the system to be produced.

We have not been able to extend our own tabulations into the succeeding years. In this section, therefore, we draw on two sources. For 1994–95, we rely on the statistical analysis provided by Professor Gillian Raab and Veronique Johnston for the Garrick Committee to bring our account slightly more up to date. Although the figures do not follow directly from our own and the institutional categories used are not exactly the same, the trends and overall picture are consistent with what we have just described in the preceding section.

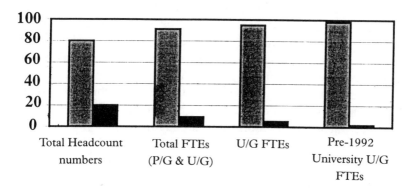

■ **Full-time**

■ **Part-time**

Figure 4.2 Participation in HE: Full-time/Part-time ratios
Source: Calculated from SOEID data

Of the 182,000 undergraduates in Scotland in 1994–95, 127, 000 attended HEIs and 54,000 further education colleges.[1] Seventy per cent attended on a full-time and 30 per cent on a part-time basis. But, as Table 4.7 shows, the sectoral distribution is very striking, with only some 4 per cent of the undergraduates in the pre-1992 universities being part-time, compared with 21 per cent of those in the new (post-1992) universities and 56 per cent of those studying at this level in further education colleges. (It should be noted, however, that, within the pre-1992 category, in the ancient universities full-timers predominate even at postgraduate level, outnumbering part-timers by two to one, but this is outweighed by the position in the old universities where the proportions are almost exactly reversed and the numbers are greater).

We have not been able to combine data from the higher and further education sectors for 1995–96. Bearing firmly in mind also the changes in data collection which make strict comparability with the earlier tables impossible, Table 4.8 presents data for 1995–96 drawn from SHEFC's own statistics for HEIs. The data show an overall total of over 30,000 for postgraduate and undergraduate part-time students – impressive enough and over 20 per cent of all such students. But let us conduct the same process which we applied to the Dearing statistics in Chapter 3. Even before that, however, it is worth noting that one institution – Strathclyde University – contributes over 5000 of those, 4510 of which are at postgraduate level. If Strathclyde's figures were around the norm for an institution of its size, the part-time total would drop by around 3000.

First, we should look separately at postgraduate and under-graduate. At postgraduate level part-timers actually out-number full-timers, with 51 per cent of the total. But at undergraduate level the proportion is 12 per cent. Then let us convert the numbers to FTEs. The overall proportion of part-timers reduces to 8 per cent – 30 per cent at postgraduate level and 5 per cent at undergraduate level. Finally, we can differentiate intra-sectorally. This shows that in the pre-1992 sector 22 per cent of all students were part-time, with 48 per cent of postgraduates but only 7 per cent of undergraduates; the equivalent figures on an FTE basis were 7 per cent, 29 per cent, and 2

---

1 Raab and Johnston rounded their numbers, which means that they do not always add up.

per cent. We can even take that figure down further: 1 in 100 of the undergraduate FTEs delivered by the ancient universities were on a part-time basis.

In short, these more recent data sustain the case we have made, namely that the part-time mode has gained no greater share of higher education provision as a whole in the massive expansion of the last decade; that it has remained almost wholly absent from the traditional heart of university provision, namely undergraduate degrees in long-established institutions; and that the numerical expansion of part-time students has been confined largely to the expansion of postgraduate provision, often as an extension of initial education for those who have just completed a full-time undergraduate degree, and to further education colleges. All these forms of provision have their own merits. We are simply making the case that there is no consistent systemic backing for part-time higher education in Scotland.[2]

---

2 See additional note in the Introduction (pp.15–17) for some recent modification
   to this position.

Chapter 5

Perspectives of Institutional Policy Makers

Introduction

In this chapter we report evidence from a series of interviews with a senior policy maker in each of the 23 Scottish HEIs (including the OU) and in 11 further education colleges. At the beginning of the project we wrote to the Principal of each institution of further or higher education in Scotland. We outlined the nature of the research, requested documentation on the institution's part-time provision and policy, and asked the Principal to nominate a senior member of the institution whom we might interview and who could speak for the institution's policy on part-time higher education. The documentation on provision was used in the analyses reported in Chapter 4. The documentation on institutional policy, which ranged from mission statements and corporate plans to internal committee papers, was used by the research team to prepare for the interviews and to complement the data collected in the interviews.

The relatively small scale of the Scottish system made it possible for us to include all HEIs in the interview study. Identifying separate institutions was not always straightforward. Some universities have a federal or semi-federal structure and some institutions have a formal link with another institution, for example as an associate college of a university, but are, nevertheless, treated by SHEFC as separate institutions for funding purposes. We decided to follow the SHEFC criterion, which led us to identify 22 separate SHEFC-funded institutions plus the OU.

We initially planned to include six to eight further education colleges in this phase of the study. However, the decision to extend the study to include HNC provision (see Chapter 3), together with a recognition of the diversity and complexity of advanced-level provision in further education, led us to select 11 colleges. These comprised a quarter of the 43 further education colleges in Scotland. They were selected to over-represent the main providers of part-time higher education, while still providing a range in respect of size, geography and mission.

As described above, the institution decided which person we should interview. In most cases the individual designated was at Vice-Principal level or equivalent, but in some cases this role was given to the person directly responsible for part-time provision, either in total or in part. Some institutions found it difficult to identify a single individual who could speak for the institution's policy on part-time higher education. This was particularly the case in institutions where decision making was substantially decentralised, especially on academic matters, and where there might be a range of faculty positions rather than a single institutional position.

The interviews were semi-structured and tape-recorded but not transcribed. Assurance of confidentiality was given, with only published information to be used in attributable fashion except where permission was given. We used the interview to check on published data and official statistics, and in several instances were able to follow up on the interview with requests for some further relevant statistics.

In presenting our data we attempt to convey the range of views expressed and, where appropriate, we refer to four of the five categories of institution introduced in Chapter 3: pre-1992 universities, post-1992 universities, non-university HEIs and further education Colleges. Although the OU was included in our interviews and the data are used in our analysis, we do not identify it in this chapter for reasons of confidentiality. In the next section we summarise our respondents' views on the costs and benefits of part-time higher education. We then go on to describe the institutions' current policy and provision, recent changes and expected future developments.

Costs and benefits of part-time higher education

Interpreting costs and benefits

We asked our interviewees what they saw as the main benefits and costs (or disadvantages) of part-time higher education to the institution and to the student respectively. Many of our interviewees had already discussed costs and benefits of part-time higher education at some length while describing their institution's policy and provision and these responses are included in the data analysed in this chapter.

Few institutions took a formal, corporate view on the costs and benefits of part-time higher education and our interviewees probably expressed their own personal views. The context of the interviews suggested that many of the views that were expressed were shared within the institution and had influenced its policies. Nevertheless, they are likely also to have reflected the personal interests and position within the institution of our interviewee. There may also have been a degree of arbitrariness concerning which of a respondent's taken-for-granted assumptions about costs and benefits were made explicit during the interview – especially, perhaps, in institutions where part-time higher education was not part of the active policy agenda. Most interviewees pointed out, or implied, that costs and benefits varied across students and institutions and depended on the mission and circumstances of the institutions, including the scale and nature of its current provision. Finally, several interviewees identified 'issues' or 'challenges' which could be interpreted as either costs or benefits according to one's point of view – for example the higher demands and expectations of part-time students, and the need for different approaches to teaching and learning.

Consequently, it would be inappropriate to draw precise, quantified conclusions about perceived costs and benefits from our interview data. Rather, the data allow us to list the main issues and criteria on which judgements of costs and benefits are based, to describe the range of perceptions in relation to each and to make cautious statements about the extent to which perceptions varied across types of institutions or according to the nature of current part-time higher education provision. In the following account we describe perceived costs and benefits under six main headings, although there is overlap across these.

Mission-oriented costs and benefits

Several interviewees pointed out that part-time higher education was a means by which the institution pursued its mission and counted this as a benefit. Part-time higher education might constitute the core business of the institution, or a significant part of it, or it might contribute towards a mission defined in terms of access, responsiveness, client-orientation, vocational or professional education or contribution to the local community. The relationship to mission was, however, not always a clear or simple one. For example, a few respondents said that part-time provision could conflict with an active research role but this was not always seen as a disadvantage – one post-1992 university linked its strong commitment to part-time provision to the low priority for research in its mission. Within the teaching mission there could also be ambiguity and tension – an interviewee at another post-1992 university perceived a potential conflict between the flexibility and individual choice which frequently accompanied part-time provision and the institution's vocational rationale which offered programmes conforming to the requirements of each relevant profession.

External links

Part-time higher education was perceived to benefit the institution by strengthening its external links. This took several forms. Some respondents, mainly in further education colleges, said that part-time provision, especially when sponsored by industry, helped the institution to maintain or improve its links with industry and employers. These links provided secondary benefits, including helping the college to keep in touch with current workplace developments and to keep its curriculum up to date, providing access to expertise and other resources, encouraging future business for the college and promoting the employment prospects of the college's full-time students. Second, several interviewees cited improved community links as a benefit of part-time higher education provision whether or not these were an explicit goal of the institution's mission. Interviewees in pre-1992 universities, including those who were not currently major providers of part-time higher education, were most likely to cite this (potential) benefit. Finally, part-time higher education can serve a public relations function for the institution, promoting awareness of the institution, enhancing its reputation for the range and diversity of its provision and encouraging future students.

Educational costs and benefits

Some of the educational costs and benefits related to the learning opportunities and experiences of part-time students. Most of our respondents stated – or at least implied – that part-time provision provided many people with opportunities for higher education which would not otherwise be available to them, particularly if they had employment or family commitments which could not easily be shed. Conversely, the experience which part-time students bring to their higher education, whether from their job or elsewhere, could enhance their learning experience as well as that of their fellow-students. However, there were also potential disadvantages. It could be difficult for part-time students to gain experience for future occupations – for example it would be hard to organise placements for part-time students in initial teacher education.

The issue of coherence also prompted opposing responses. On the one hand, some felt that part-time study – especially when associated with modularisation – would threaten the integrity of the student experience. A policy maker in an art college linked this experience with the 'hothouse' nature of the institution:

> The real strength of [the college] is ... in the hands-on unlimited access to your workplace and the development of the individual as a creative person. It is not just a series of pieces of information that students gather ... [with more flexible provision] we would be merely educating and training a bigger number of people in more flexible ways, but we wouldn't actually have the kind of success that we have had in producing top designers, top artists and top architects.

Others identified problems of coherence with student choice rather than with the part-time nature of a course. The director of a university CATs programme expressed the contrary view:

> There is nothing wrong with the cafeteria approach because people do choose sensibly what they are eating. We don't have tomato sauce on top of our ice cream .... The coherence is in the eye of the student.

Several respondents referred to the social dimension of the student experience. Some, especially in the pre-1992 universities, felt that part-time study could not supply the personal and social dimension of higher education which was gained through university and college life:

> What is lacking completely is the social element. We have come to the conclusion that we will be able to give our full-time students a university education, but for those who are doing part-time or flexible learning all that we can probably hope for is to give them a high quality university training.

However, some felt that this view was premised on an Oxbridge institutional environment and ignored the realities of modern student life:

I've got one student with psychiatric problems coming to see me today. She's working 15 hours a day to earn her keep and it's just that she is broken down.

The overall composition of the student body was a further factor. A common response, especially in universities, referred to part-time provision as a means of attracting 'good' students or achieving a better student mix. It could attract high-ability students, especially from disadvantaged areas, or students whose maturity and experience would enhance the learning experience of fellow students and the ethos and atmosphere of the institution as a whole.

Finally, the issue of quality of provision was raised, with several aspects. One concerned the expectations and demands of part-time students, which could be perceived as a cost or a benefit. Part-time students or their employers are more likely to be the direct customers for their courses and many have made considerable personal sacrifices to study. They are less likely to accept a poor quality of provision. While few respondents said that part-time provision was of lower quality than full-time provision, several, mostly in the pre-1992 universities, identified certain challenges that it raised. These concerned the measurement and comparability of standards, particularly in the context of flexible and distance learning and in relation to the recognition and transfer of credit (especially where grades were involved). Lastly, part-time study may require a different approach to teaching and learning, and in institutions where provision is integrated this has implications for provision for full-time students.

Personal costs and benefits

We have already described some of the educational benefits to part-time students, not least that part-time provision provides opportunities for higher education which might not otherwise be available to them. Several respondents said that students might derive other personal benefits, including career and personal development (for example gains in self-confidence). Some said that part-time students tended to be isolated and not to be involved in college or university life and suggested that this was a personal cost, although others pointed out that part-time students often developed their own social support networks and some derived benefit from the social life it could provide. Our respondents were generally reluctant to speculate in detail about personal costs and benefits for students but, predictably enough, they mentioned the following as likely factors: finance, time pressures, impact on personal life and relationships, and motivation.

Costs and benefits for staff

Especially in further education, part-time courses were seen to benefit staff by enabling them to establish or strengthen contact with employers and thereby to keep up to date with developments in the world of work. More generally, the contact with motivated and mature students was seen as a benefit. However, to the extent that part-time provision involved teaching in the evening or at weekends, this was likely to be perceived as a cost.

There are wider contractual and employment issues. For example, in one post-1992 university we were told of the rules governing the deployment of staff. Staff are employed on terms which lay down a global annual figure of working hours, about 1300, with a 40-week year. Thirty of the 32.5 hours in the week are at the employer's discretion, with 108 hours in the year to be deployed by the employer for teaching outside the 'normal' day. In the institution where we had the most detailed discussion of this, the 'normal' day was defined as 8 am to 6 pm. Clearly, this is a major, and sensitive, area which needs further exploration.

Resources

It was not possible to explore in detail the resource implications of policy developments in any institution. The only instance where it was possible even to conjure with figures was where a Flexibility In Teaching and Learning Scheme (FITLS) grant from SHEFC was explicitly cited as enabling expansion into part-time higher education to occur, and this led on to a discussion of internal resource allocation, but even here the picture was not fully defined. All we can do here is list the items or issues which were mentioned as having resource implications:

- The most significant item was the use of part-time provision as a way of accomplishing expansion and thereby attracting public funding when full-time places are capped. How such expansion actually benefits an institution will vary – in some cases through more intensive use of capacity, in others by bringing in income.

- Development costs were cited. These covered capital expenditure on varying scales, from establishing distance learning provision or outreach centres to relatively minor costs, staff development and curriculum development.

- Student numbers constitute another angle. On the one hand, part-time students could be seen as infill, making up numbers at a very low marginal cost. On the other hand, putting on a part-time class could be costly if the numbers were not sufficient (as with any class).

- Overhead costs refer to heating, lighting and administration. Where part-time means evening provision, there could be additional costs if buildings were not otherwise to be open.

- Short-term v. long-term costs was a final consideration. In some cases there were references to start-up costs which would be expected to diminish over time, in others there could be instances where initial costs are covered by pump-priming funding which then disappears.

Other than at the level of the individual course, we were not presented with evidence of precise formulae for calculating resource costs. This does not mean that they are not seriously monitored but, in most instances, they are likely to be part of a wider institutional budgeting process which does not allow specific bottom-line judgements to be made.

Interviewees' perceptions of the costs and benefits of part-time higher education varied across institutions. This variation reflected differences in the traditions, ethos and missions of institutions as well as in their funding and organisation and in the types and levels of courses they provided.

Nevertheless, there was substantial consensus on the general costs and benefits of part-time higher education, even if respondents varied in the extent to which they felt these did or should apply to their own institution. The main area of disagreement concerned the holistic nature of the educational experience. Some respondents felt that part-time courses tended to be fragmented and lack coherence. Others questioned the concept of coherence that underlay this view and pointed out that part-time students could often integrate their learning with other practical or work experience to a greater extent than full-time students. Some claimed that part-timers missed some of the broader social experiences that were an important feature of higher education. Others questioned whether this model of higher education was still applicable to most full-time students.

Resource-related issues were important for institutions' judgements of the costs and benefits of part-time higher education. In the further education sector, the introduction of the funding methodology based on SUMS (Student Units of Measurement) had removed disincentives to part-time provision. This had clearly influenced several colleges. Resource considerations were central to planning at the institutional and strategic levels. However, they are not only highly complex, they are also highly variable in relation to the institution, the subjects, the level and type of courses, the context of other provision and so on. Despite having discussed the issue with all the institutional policy makers in our study, we find it impossible to generalise about it. While funding is clearly a very powerful instrument of policy, the complexity and variability of resource considerations means that it may also be a very blunt one.

Expansion and flexibility: institutional policies for part-time higher education

The status of institutional policies

In our interviews we asked about each institution's current policy for part-time higher education, whether this had changed in the last few years and, if so, the reasons for the changes. The responses reflected the increasing mission-consciousness of both HEIs and further education colleges. When discussing their institutions' policies for part-time higher education, nearly all interviewees related it to their perceptions of the institutional mission, whether or not this was articulated in a mission statement. According to our interviewees, policy on part-time higher education was made – or at least co-ordinated – at the top level of most institutions, rather than being dependent on initiatives at departmental or divisional level. This may, of course, reflect the perspective of our interviewees, who were chosen to represent institutional-level policy making.

In several institutions 'policy' for part-time higher education was passive or implicit. In HEIs where part-time provision was currently low and there were no plans to expand it, it was not part of the explicit policy agenda. As one interviewee put it, 'the fact that there isn't a demand means we don't leave first base' in considering part-time provision; 'we don't have a unit which plans for part-time education'. However, the same institution had been considering distance learning in another context and our interviewee recognised that 'if we were really struggling we would have to re-think the whole thing'. Conversely, part-time higher education was so central to the current mission and practice of some other institutions that no formal policy – in the usual sense which connotes an intended change in practice – was felt to be necessary. Even where institutions were embarking on a considered course of expansion, their interviewees found it hard to define the status of the decisions that led to it. Asked whether his institution (a pre-1992 university) had a policy for part-time provision, one interviewee replied 'Yes, I think so. If not, we're only just short of it. It depends how you interpret committee minutes'.

Even when institutions pursued active policies which affected part-time provision, these were not necessarily framed in terms of part-time higher education as such. For example, many further education colleges had a policy to increase advanced-level provision. When full-time advanced provision was 'capped', colleges sought to expand part-time provision instead, but this was not how the policy had originally been defined. Several HEIs had active policies on part-time postgraduate courses or continuing education. These policies might spill over into undergraduate provision, the subject of our research, but they were less clearly articulated for this level. Nearly all the institutions we visited framed their policies in terms of overarching concepts such as flexibility and responsiveness. Part-time study was an aspect of this but not necessarily one for which specific policy was made.

In discussing institutional policies for part-time higher education we must, therefore, take account of the extent to which these policies were implicit or were not explicitly framed in relation to part-time higher education. Allowing for this, we can identify two prevailing thrusts of policy: a quantitative thrust which focused on expansion and a qualitative thrust which focused on flexibility. We discuss these below.

Expansion: policies for the level of part-time higher education provision

All the further education colleges we visited aimed to expand their provision of part-time higher education. These included two small colleges with no formal policy but *de facto* expansion plans and two or three colleges which planned to expand provision across the board, not specifically in relation to part-time higher education. We did not visit colleges with little or no advanced provision. But among colleges currently offering some part-time higher education, most planned to increase this offer – some by increasing the range of part-time HNCs and developing post-HNC provision, for example professional development awards, others by focusing their expansion plans on HNDs and, in some of the largest colleges, by introducing or expanding degree-level provision.

All post-1992 universities planned substantial expansion in part-time higher education provision. Those whose provision was already substantial aimed to increase it and those with less developed provision planned large increases. As we have seen in Chapter 4, post-1992 universities account for a large proportion of part-time degree students and for most of the part-time higher education located in HEIs. If the policy intentions revealed in our interviews are fulfilled, they are likely to retain and even increase this market share.

Among the pre-1992 universities the picture is more mixed. One aimed to expand provision which was already well developed; three had policies to expand, more or less gradually, from lower starting points; and the other four reported no formal policy. Usually, this meant that there were no plans to expand provision, which was currently low, although in two cases policy reviews were imminent.

Current part-time provision by the non-university HEIs was low and only one had plans to expand it. Another had recently reversed expansion plans. Two others reported policies for enhancing individualised provision and access respectively, and this might involve an increase in part-time opportunities, but any increase would be small in the near future.

Taken together, if the policy goals reported in our interviews are realised, the provision of part-time higher education in Scotland will expand substantially in the next few years. Much of the expansion will occur among institutions which are already relatively large providers, especially the post-1992 universities. The further education sector will increase its aggregate share of part-time higher education provision, but our sample of further education colleges does not easily allow us to make statements about differences within the further education sector.

Flexibility: policies for the organisation of part-time higher education provision

Several institutions had policies, not for part-time higher education as such but for a more flexible pattern of provision in which part-time study was likely to form a significant component. Notions of flexibility permeated our interviews. As we discussed in Chapter 2, there are several dimensions to the concept of flexibility and our interviewees used the term in several different senses. It was variously linked with other concepts and policy objectives such as openness, access, responsiveness and diversity. While there was considerable variation in the concept of flexibility across institutions within each sector, we perceived the largest difference to lie between universities and further education colleges.

Most universities which wanted to expand part-time provision pursued a model of *flexible integration*. This might include: modularisation and credit-rating of courses; a single timetable for full- and part-time students, usually based on an extension of the 'normal' day; formal access of all students to all units, subject to specific entry requirements; a CATs or Combined Studies programme; the 'blocking' of the timetable to facilitate part-time study of the most popular programmes; duplication of particular courses or units in the evenings and on Saturdays; making key units available to full- and part-time students through flexible learning; longer opening hours for facilities; and special support (and, sometimes, admission) arrangements for part-time students. The flexible integration strategy aimed to provide what one interviewee termed a 'seamless environment' of full- and part-time study and to place the main emphasis on making existing provision accessible to all students on as 'part-time-friendly' a basis as possible.

No university's policy represented a pure type of the flexible integration model. Conversely, many elements of the model were also implied in the policies pursued by further education colleges. However, we perceived that, at least as a matter of emphasis, the colleges' policies more closely approximated a model of *flexible differentiation*. This model places more emphasis on the diversity of provision and the need to respond to the diverse needs of the market. Thus further education colleges were more likely to see the future of part-time higher education provision in terms of customised programmes for specific employers, delivery in the workplace and other off-campus delivery.

While we would stress that the difference between flexible integration and flexible differentiation is a matter of emphasis and degree, we believe that two general factors explain this difference between the sectors. The first is the stronger imperative for further education colleges to be responsive to their markets – flexible differentiation is a demand-driven policy, whereas flexible integration is at least partly concerned with rationalising supply. The second factor is the different nature of the sectors' markets – further education, with its tradition of day-release and employer-sponsored courses, and with HNCs rather than degrees accounting for most of its provision, has a more segmented market which is more dependent on particular employers.

Factors influencing policy

Interviewees' reasons for institutional policies and, in particular, for recent policy changes, referred to three sets of factors: those specific to the institution, government policy and funding, and demand.

INSTITUTION-SPECIFIC FACTORS
MISSION

Several institutions, especially those which planned to expand their part-time higher education provision, gave 'mission-related' reasons for their policies. These generally referred to the institution's commitment to access, openness or responsiveness, to its vocational or community orientation or to the absence of a strong research orientation. These reasons tended to be similar across institutions, as far as our semi-structured interview data allow us to judge, with two main exceptions. First, the non-university HEIs were more likely to refer to student-centred or individualist reasons for increasing flexibility, although most had little scope for increasing part-time provision in practice. Second, the post-1992 universities were much more likely than other institutions to give mission-oriented reasons for their policies. All five interviewees in post-1992 universities gave such reasons, compared with a minority within each other category of institution. We can only speculate whether this reflects a real difference in policy making or whether leaders of the post-1992 universities were simply more self-conscious about the role and mission of their institutions following their recent change in status. If it is a real difference, this suggests that the post-1992 universities are more committed to their role as providers of part-time higher education than other institutions and, perhaps, more confident about its expediency.

ABILITY AND NEED TO EXPAND

Nearly all the institutions in our study wished to expand student numbers. This goal underpinned many of the other policy considerations discussed in this chapter but it was rarely made explicit in the interview – it is part of the taken-for-granted reality of institutional policy. It was only made explicit by institutions whose circumstances put them at the two extremes of the spectrum. At one extreme some post-1992 universities felt that expansion was an organisational imperative as they were currently too small to be viable. At the other extreme several non-university HEIs were unable to expand, either because of resource constraints (for example the Art Colleges) or because student numbers within their specialist fields were limited (for example initial teacher education). If demand for full-time student places already exceeded this constrained supply, institutions saw little point in introducing or increasing part-time provision.

CRITICAL MASS: THE SCALE OF EXISTING PROVISION

In some HEIs there was little current part-time provision and its expansion would represent a major qualitative change. In others part-time provision was already substantial and further expansion would primarily involve a quantitative change. The former required some additional factor – such as development funding or very committed institutional leadership – to get part-time provision off the ground. Some non-university HEIs were cutting out their existing part-time provision because it was too small to be viable.

CHANGES IN INSTITUTIONAL STRUCTURE AND CONTROL

In some HEIs and further education colleges the arrival of a new Principal had been an important catalyst. In addition to such personal factors, several colleges had recently restructured, typically creating a smaller number of divisions which more closely matched the changed labour market and the demand for further education courses. This was also seen as a catalyst for policy change. Interviewees in several further education colleges said that the colleges' incorporation in 1993 had stimulated change. It had enabled them to develop new provision more rapidly and had removed the constraints of education authority policies which sought to rationalise provision across local institutions. It had also made colleges more customer-conscious and more responsive. However, some interviewees pointed out that incorporation merely reinforced changes which were already under way and that advanced-level participation in further education colleges took off before incorporation.

MODULARISATION, CREDIT-RATING AND SEMESTERISATION

Modularisation and credit transfer had, for several years, been part of the taken-for-granted world of further education colleges. Most HEIs had either introduced, or were currently planning, modular course structures, typically as part of a broader strategy for flexibility. All HEIs are members of the SCOTCAT scheme, although, in some cases, this had little impact on practices within the institution. Several HEIs had also introduced semesters.

The three processes – modularisation, credit-rating (and accumulation) and semesterisation – tended to be closely linked in the policies of the institutions that we studied. However, they were not always linked in the same way, nor were the terms used consistently by our respondents. For example, some used the term 'unit' rather than 'module' to connote the continued integrity of the course or programme and/or the variable size of units. This makes it difficult to generalise about the impact of modularisation, or of related processes, on part-time provision. Nevertheless, our data make it clear that while modularisation, credit-rating and semesterisation do not necessarily result in an expansion of part-time provision, they may all have a powerful catalytic or facilitating effect. This effect may be understood in terms of their contribution to the model of flexible integration which underpinned most institutions' expansion plans. Semesterisation adds a further dimension to this model by providing greater flexibility in the pace of study (especially where a third semester is provided), allowing two or three entry points during the year and opening up a new mode of part-time study in which semesters of full-time study alternate with semesters back on the job or elsewhere.

They thus reduced the 'threshold cost' of offering part-time provision in institutions where it was currently small or negligible, and even in the pre-1992 universities where part-time provision was negligible it was acknowledged that modularisation might be a catalyst for further change. Conversely, going a little beyond our data, we would speculate that it is increasingly difficult for an institution to offer part-time higher education except on the basis of a modular course structure, probably credit-rated and possibly semesterised.

TECHNOLOGY/DISTANCE LEARNING

A very few institutions had already invested fairly heavily and aimed to build on this in developing policies for flexible and/or part-time provision.

OTHER FACTORS

In the previous chapter we analysed the costs and benefits of part-time higher education as perceived by our respondents. Some of these were used to explain current institutional policies – for example the difficulties of providing appropriate work experience for some vocational courses was a reason for not developing part-time provision.

GOVERNMENT POLICY AND FUNDING

The second set of factors influencing policy arose from the mechanisms and policies for funding higher education.

FUNDING ARRANGEMENTS

The broad context of funding and control had a pronounced influence on the way in which institutions went about making policy. Several interviewees in further education colleges said that incorporation had made colleges more market- and customer-oriented. This contributed indirectly to policies for expanding part-time provision. (However, colleges' missions and policies varied widely with respect to 'non-market' goals such as support for the community and the alleviation of disadvantage.) An interviewee in a college of education described the change in thinking which followed the move to SHEFC funding. Under the old (Scottish Office Education Department-funded) system the college did 'good works' such as in-service training, curriculum development and work for the Examination Board:

Each year you wrote and said what you did and they said 'good on you, and here's the money for next year'. Under the regime of the SHEFC we're forced by all kinds of things ... because we're in a different regime, because money is tight, we are working on formula funding ... and so on. That has triggered a different kind of thinking in the College and a lot of the recent expansion ideas have been fuelled from the kind of imperatives that are coming from the Funding Council.

None of our interviewees in the post-1992 universities cited the move to university status as a major factor behind their expansion of part-time provision – somewhat surprisingly, in view of their leading role in the planned expansion.

FUNDING POLICIES AND FORMULAE

For most further education colleges which planned to expand part-time higher education provision, the single most important reason was that funding policies – the 'capping' policy announced in 1994 – restricted the opportunity to expand full-time higher education. Usually, our interviewees implied that otherwise they would have preferred to expand full-time provision or at least offer a different mix of full-time and part-time. Consolidation policies had had a similar impact on HEIs, although this was mentioned less consistently by our interviewees in these institutions. In both sectors interviewees commented on the change in relative funding formulae for full-time and part-time courses, in favour of the latter, although there was disagreement as to whether the existing differential adequately allowed for the differences in the costs of provision.

'MAINSTREAMING' OF CONTINUING EDUCATION FUNDING

The pre-1992 universities which currently receive SHEFC funding for continuing personal education (liberal adult education) faced the prospect of this funding being integrated into funding for mainstream provision and tied to the accreditation of provision. Our interviewees in some of the pre-1992 universities felt that the new policy was not yet clear enough for a specific policy to emerge in response. Potentially, it could result in large numbers of additional students coming to be counted as part-time undergraduate students and in students using credits gained in continuing education to count towards mainstream qualifications. However, even those institutions which anticipated the new funding regime most proactively were very uncertain as to whether this would lead to the full integration of continuing education provision with mainstream undergraduate provision and this uncertainty remains at the time of writing.

DEVELOPMENT SUPPORT

Specific development funding, such as the FITLS, had often played a critical role in getting part-time higher education off the ground, especially in the pre-1992 universities.

PERCEIVED DIRECTION OF POLICY

Funding arrangements were a major influence on institutions' policies for part-time higher education. Nevertheless, institutions responded, not only to the incentives and constraints implied in current funding formulae but also to the government policy intentions that were perceived to lie behind them. The planning process encouraged this – especially in the further education sector, which receives its funding directly from the Scottish Office without an intermediary Funding Council. As one interviewee in an further education college noted, 'it would be foolish not to take cognisance of the way that policies are being directed'. Like others in the sector, he perceived a policy thrust favouring the part-time route for colleges' advanced provision. This did not always lead to the same outcome, however. Another college manager commented:

> To some extent … [certain colleges] have become, in effect, university colleges, which wasn't well received by the Scottish Office, so our route has been somewhat different.

The post-1992 universities also perceived strong policy encouragement for the expansion of part-time education. Nevertheless, the signals conveyed by the government and SHEFC were not always clear:

> Are we [HEIs] competing with one another or are we collaborating with one another? … No one has got the answer to that right because of the conflicting signals that we get.

DEMAND

The final set of factors influencing policy was the perceived demand from students or other 'customers'. Institutions responded to the perceived trend in demand for their full-time or non-advanced provision, on the one hand, and for part-time higher education on the other. Demand for part-time courses also had a strong local dimension.

DEMAND FOR OTHER PROVISION WITHIN THE INSTITUTION

Several universities were encouraged to expand part-time provision by fears of a decline in the demand for full-time courses. Some reported a fall-off after the recent period of rising applications. While some universities felt more vulnerable than others, even those where student demand remained buoyant on average voiced concerns about particular subjects and departments. Two factors lay behind the anxieties about student demand: the declining flow of school leavers due to demographic trends and the rising financial cost of full-time study, which it was felt would deter participation. However, this was not an area where predictions were made with certainty. One of the largest providers of part-time higher education had expanded its provision in the early 1990s because it anticipated a decline in full-time demand following the demographic downturn. This decline had not materialised, with resulting pressure on resources.

Institutions in both further education and higher education sectors were aware of pressures from full-time students who needed to work long hours to finance themselves. Many had responded by modifying the timetable, for example by concentrating classes in the three middle days of each week and allowing the other days free for employment. Full-time provision was thus being made more 'flexible' and some respondents commented on how this was weakening the boundary between full- and part-time study. However, funding arrangements, both for institutions and for students, still acted to maintain this boundary, although some respondents perceived signs of flexibility. One respondent in an further education college felt that the Student Awards Agency for Scotland showed flexibility in the definition of full-time study, allowing deviations from normal full-time hours for students with special needs. He suggested that the Agency might be equally disposed to look favourably on other students seeking flexibility.

DEMAND FOR PART-TIME HIGHER EDUCATION

Most respondents in further education reported a recent decline in employer demand for day-release provision, which was still the largest type of part-time provision for most colleges. Some colleges hoped for a recovery but there was a general feeling that past levels of demand would not return. There were also more qualitative changes, described by one respondent (whose courses served an industry previously noted for its conservatism) as a 'culture change' among employers. They were increasingly demanding programmes tailored to their particular requirements, sometimes preferring individual HN units rather than complete programmes. There was a trend towards on-site delivery. There was also a shift from the employer towards the individual student as the customer for further education provision. For example, day-release was sometimes moving towards a half-day-plus-evening pattern, with students matching their employer's contribution with their own time, or students might be expected to start a course in the evening and be permitted release from work once they have demonstrated an initial commitment.

These changes help to explain the move towards flexibility in higher education provision but they do not in themselves suggest that there will be a market for the significant expansion of part-time provision that both further education colleges and HEIs are planning. Our respondents offered three main reasons for anticipating increased demand. First, some believed that there were untapped areas of demand – including a demand for the more 'flexible' forms of provision described above. Second, some perceived an upgrading in employers' demands – for example one reported that the market for National Certificates had 'collapsed' and employers now expected HN qualifications. This view was expressed most often in respect of certain subject areas (for example business and administration) and relatively buoyant labour markets. Third, several respondents anticipated a future society characterised by frequent job change and lifelong learning in which people would move in and out of higher education over the life cycle.

LOCAL DIMENSION TO DEMAND

Cross-cutting these issues was the local dimension. Some HEIs felt their local populations were too small to sustain a demand for part-time courses – if they offered part-time provision it tended to be provided either by distance learning or as short residential courses. All institutions took account of the size of their local catchment and the existing part-time provision offered by other local institutions. However, except for the various forms of further education-higher education links, we found little evidence of active collaboration among institutions to share markets or avoid duplication.

Institutional and sectoral differences in policy influences

Do the policies described above indicate a trend towards institutional differentiation or convergence in Scottish higher education? Our evidence is mixed. On the one hand, most institutions are developing or expanding part-time higher education provision and the few institutions that are not doing so are taking the idea more seriously than in the past. In this respect there appears to be convergence. On the other hand, institutions vary in their rate of expansion and in their commitment to expansion. The trends revealed by our study suggest that the post-1992 universities may actually increase their already substantial share of part-time first degree provision. Within the further education sector, the expansion of part-time advanced courses in some further education colleges may increase the gap between these colleges and others which offer little or no advanced provision.

Within the higher education sector, institutions whose current part-time provision was small found it difficult to generate the critical mass of resources and infrastructure required to expand it cost-effectively. Some non-university HEIs had withdrawn part-time provision precisely for this reason. This supply-side inertia may encourage continued diversity in the provision of part-time opportunities. However, institutions which have introduced credit-rating, modularisation and semesterisation have found that the threshold cost of introducing significant part-time provision is significantly reduced. As these aspects of flexibility are introduced to more HEIs, and in progressively stronger forms, perhaps we may see future institutional convergence, with part-time provision playing a larger part in the policies of all or most institutions.

However, convergence in this sense – towards a position where most institutions offer part-time opportunities – may not entail institutional convergence in any broader sense. There continue to be strong functional differences between further education colleges and HEIs reflected in the different funding regimes and policy environments, the different levels of courses offered (with the emphasis on HNC/HND and degree provision respectively) and, to some extent, the different modes of provision – what we have referred to as flexible differentiation and flexible integration. And among HEIs, part-time opportunities can be developed in pursuit of very different missions. The provision of part-time higher education may cut across other dimensions of institutional differentiation – that is, institutions pursuing very different missions may still recognise a need to organise some of their provision on a part-time basis. Indeed, there may even be a contrary relationship: the greater the institutional diversity, the greater the need for all (or most) institutions to offer part-time provision, given that there is a need for part-time opportunities within most types of provision.

Emerging issues

Our research was based on the importance of institutional policies for the future provision of part-time higher education. Yet our interviewees almost unanimously reported that institutional policies were substantially driven by funding and by markets. Many of them gave voice to a sense of institutional powerlessness. A university Vice-Principal said: 'It's hard to be in control. We've managed so far but it may get harder in the future'. There was little room to manoeuvre with a declining unit of resource – it was hard to make long-term policy when the market was uncertain and the funding regime liable to change. A respondent in a college pointed out that 'policy and implementing that policy are not the same thing' – the college may put together a three-year development plan but the funding goalposts might change during that period and the college would have to change tack very quickly. Such comments call into question the concept of institutional autonomy and also the notion of mission-driven change. At best, institutional policies and missions may be little more than rationalisations of positions which institutions are forced to adopt by external pressures. In this view, the shift from 'planning inputs' to 'auditing outcomes' (Scott 1995) does not represent a diminution of government control but simply a changed mode of control.

This raises a further issue. If institutions are not really in control, or at least stand ready to change tack if the winds should change, how well entrenched are institutional policies? How much importance should we attach to their current policy statements and to the trends – the expansion and flexibilisation of part-time higher education – which these policies promised to bring about?

The interviews gave us grounds for scepticism. The policies that were described to us were recent and many institutions had already changed their policies. Some had already restrained their expansion plans in response to changing perceptions of demand or to changes in funding and resource imperatives. Some institutions' commitment to part-time higher education may not have been very strong – several had chosen to expand part-time higher education in response to the capping or consolidation of full-time provision. If these policies were removed, the implication is that part-time provision might again take lower priority. A further implication is that the differentiation of provision across institutions will be greater than indicated in our interviews since policies for part-time expansion seemed much better entrenched in some institutions than in others.

A further cause for scepticism arises from the contrast between the careful market research which informed the development of some courses and the much more speculative extrapolations of social and economic trends which informed longer-term strategy. Many respondents were uncertain about the longer-term prospects – this uncertainty arose variously from economic trends, especially in depressed local labour markets, from employers' growing reluctance to sponsor part-time students and from a fear that part-time provision may be drawing from a finite pool of potential students which would eventually be drained.

The policies for flexibility espoused by most institutions often assumed a progressive erosion of the boundaries between full- and part-time study. Here again a sceptic might question whether this erosion was imminent or, at least, whether it might be progressing in geological rather than educational time. The demand for flexibility will be constrained by continuing sources of rigidity arising from student funding regulations, institutional funding procedures and the nature of employer demand (in particular the importance of traditional day-release and the growth of on-site provision, which tend to require dedicated part-time provision).

Our scepticism may be unjustified. Changes in these factors could accelerate the erosion or even cause the boundaries to collapse together. Our interviews revealed several instances where institutions, once they had developed part-time provision, acquired a strong commitment to its continuation where student demand for part-time higher education continued to outstrip the supply of full-time provision and where a flexible pattern of provision was the basis for sustained expansion. There may be a wider logic favouring flexibility and expansion in part-time higher education, but, if so, this logic rests upon something stronger than institutional missions.

Chapter 6

Part-Time Provision in Four Institutions

The case studies

Selecting the institutions to study

In this chapter we continue the institutional level of analysis but we look in more detail at our four case study institutions and at the eight courses – two in each institution – on which we focused our research. We start by describing how we selected the institutions and how we collected our data within them. We then describe the eight part-time courses or programmes. We take advantage of the diverse experience covered by the case studies to discuss some more general issues in the provision of part-time higher education, focusing first at the institutional level and then at the level of course or programme. The following chapters present further evidence from the case studies. Chapter 7 describes part-time students, their backgrounds, their aspirations and their reasons for studying. Chapter 8 discusses the experience of part-time study, how students manage it in relation to their work and family commitments, and the costs and benefits of part-time study for students. Finally, Chapter 9 discusses relationships with employers.

In selecting the case study institutions we wanted to include one pre-1992 university, one post-1992 university, a large further education college and a small college. We wanted to choose institutions which had a significant number of part-time students and offered a variety of part-time courses or programmes at advanced or first degree level. This simplified the selection of higher education institutions, several of which had little in the way of part-time provision other than at postgraduate level or in continuing education or extra-mural departments. However, among colleges there is more of a continuum with respect to part-time advanced courses – some colleges have very substantial provision and others virtually none, with colleges are at various intermediate positions on the continuum. We wanted to capture some of this variation, so we chose one large college which was well established as a large-scale provider of part-time advanced (mainly HNC) courses and a small college with much less experience at this level. We also wanted to cover a variety of local demographic factors (whether the institution was located in an urban or rural setting and the size of its catchment area), modes of attendance (evening only, day-release or mixed mode) and modes of provision (dedicated part-time classes or integration with full-time classes).

Taking all these things into consideration, we selected four institutions. We wrote to their Principals inviting them to participate in this phase of the research, and some were later visited by members of the project team to discuss in more detail what the case studies would entail. Permission was subsequently given by each Principal. In order to honour the project team's assurances of confidentiality and anonymity, we avoid naming institutions and henceforward we will refer to them as college A (small further education college), college B (large college), university C (post-1992) and university D (pre-1992). In each institution there were two main strands to the research: a survey of part-time students and studies of two courses or programmes based on interviews with staff, students, employers and family members.

The student survey

The first research strand was a student survey. This was based on a self-completion questionnaire sent during March 1996 to a sample of 250 part-time higher education students in each institution. In three institutions we attempted to sample students in at least their second year of study. In the fourth institution, which had fewer than 250 part-time higher education students, we sampled all part-time students. In addition, 250 questionnaires were sent to a sample of OU students based in the Scottish region in order to compare and contrast their experiences.

The institutions were understandably reluctant to release the names and addresses of their students, so they agreed to send out the questionnaires on our behalf. This meant that the institutions were also responsible for selecting the samples, following criteria and procedures which we had specified. These arrangements were an appropriate compromise between the interests of the research and the legitimate confidentiality concerns of the institutions, but they represented a loss of control by the research team. The sample

Table 6.1 Rate of return, by institution (percentages)

Institution	Rate of return (%)
College A	29
College B	42
University C	51
University D	46
Open University	67

selection procedures fell short of the strict criteria of probability sampling which are regarded as the norm in social science research. Moreover, although questionnaires were returned directly to the research team, the fact that they were sent out by the institution may have encouraged a higher response among students favourably disposed towards the institution. As with the interviews described below, there may have been a slight bias towards optimism in our sampling and data-collection procedures.

Each student in the sample received a package containing an A4 leaflet describing the research, a letter inviting them to participate in the research, a questionnaire and a prepaid return envelope. The questionnaire ran to 16 pages of mainly structured questions. Some two or three weeks later they received reminder postcards.

Response rates from each institution are shown in Table 6.1. The rate of return in college A was considerably lower than in the other institutions. Several interviewees in college A commented on the time pressures on a number of students but we can only speculate that this contributed to the low response. We designed the sample to be representative of the subject areas of part-time students. Within each subject area allocation the gender balance was roughly proportional to the institution's student profile. Table 6.2 summarises the level and

**Table 6.2 Students' level of study and subject, by sector
(percentages)**

	Universities	Colleges	OU
Level of study			
HNC	0	81	0
HND	0	6	0
Degree	93	1	99
Other	6	12	1
Subject			
Arts	7	0	19
Maths/Science	38	10	38
Social Sciences	23	5	36
Art & Design	2	3	1
Business/Law	15	26	1
Engineering	14	55	7
Sample n (=100%)	243	145	168

subject of study of the students who responded, as reported in the questionnaires.

Interviews

The second strand of the case study research involved in-depth interviews with staff, students and, where possible, employers and families of students. We also carried out group discussions with students. We conducted most of the interviews in college A, college B and university D between April and June 1996, and in university C between June and August 1996.

This strand of the research focused on two courses or programmes selected from within each institution, eight courses in all. As will be seen from the descriptions below, the definition of a course or programme proved somewhat arbitrary, especially where course structures were flexible or where a department offered different specialisms within the same course. A minimum criterion was that the course should be available throughout the academic year, over two semesters or three terms or sessions. In selecting these courses we aimed to cover a wide spectrum of subjects, modes of attendance and levels of study. Other contrasts also influenced the selection of courses – for example male or female subject areas, newness or longevity of courses and varying relationships with employers and local industry.

We wrote to the eight department heads or programme organisers for the selected courses asking for permission to conduct the research. We subsequently visited them to explain the team's requirements in more detail and to answer any queries. In one case the head of department wrote back to advise us that all the relevant staff involved with part-time teaching would be on leave or on sabbatical during the period when the interviews were to be carried out. Fortunately, a replacement course was found at short notice from within the same broad subject grouping. The courses or programmes studied, and the range of interviews conducted for each, are summarised in Table 6.3.

Our interviews with staff covered at least four different categories of staff. First, department heads, or their equivalent, with formal responsibility for departmental policies on part-time provision and delivery and input into institutional policies; they may also have taught on part-time courses. Second, course leaders or co-ordinators who normally undertook most of the administrative duties in relation to the part-time course or programme, most of whom also had some

Table 6.3 Interviews, by institution and course

Course	Staff	Student	Employer	Family	Group
College A					
HNC Engineering	2	6	1	1	1*
HNC Social Care	4	6	3**	1	1
College B					
HNC Accounting	4	5	2	0	1
HNC Graphic Design	3	5	2	0	1
University C					
Combined Studies	3†	6	0	0	0
Health Studies	2†	5	0	0	0
University D					
Business Studies	3	5	0	0	1
English Studies	4	5	0	0	1
PTDO††	1	–	–	–	–

*   The group discussion was conducted with infill Automotive
       Engineering students.
**   Includes one telephone interview.
†   Includes one member of staff who had been involved with the
       establishment of both programmes in University C.
††   Part-Time Degree Office

teaching involvement. Third, lecturers or tutors who were largely responsible for delivery and internal assessment of courses. Finally, part-time staff who were mostly bought in to undertake (often specialised) teaching or tutorial assistance tasks, almost invariably for evening classes.

To maintain the confidentiality of student records, most student interviewees were recruited by staff whom we had previously interviewed. In a few cases we were allowed to address meetings of the class and recruit volunteers. In addition to individual interviews, group discussions were held with students from six of the eight courses. All members of the project team were involved with the interview programme – each of us interviewed singly or in pairs in at least three of the four institutions.

During the student interviews, if it emerged that the student was employed and that their employer was making any contribution towards the student's fees, we asked for permission to approach their employer to request an interview. Unsurprisingly, recruitment of employers was most successful on courses with strong vocational links and we interviewed one or two employers in relation to each of the college courses. We were unable to secure employer interviews from any of the university courses, although two of these courses did have clear vocational links. In university D most of those students who were employer-funded were employees of the university itself, while in university C the 'employers' for one of the programmes tended to be large public-sector organisations and it was difficult to find an appropriate representative to be interviewed. In a brief follow-up piece of fieldwork we conducted interviews with representatives of the universities as employers (see Chapter 9).

If the student did not live alone, we also sought permission to interview family or household members. In the event, we only interviewed a very few family members. Some student interviewees lived alone, others were unwilling for their families to be approached and, in a few cases, the domestic circumstances which had been described during interviews suggested that a family interview would be either intrusive or inappropriate. Time factors proved a further constraint – it normally took much longer to arrange and conduct an interview with a family member than with a student or member of staff.

To analyse the interview data we defined a thematic grid which identified key themes and topics with each theme. This grid was used to provide an analytic portrait of each institution in turn. The process was iterative: the grid was modified or expanded to accommodate themes arising from each case study to which it was applied. We then placed the four institutional portraits alongside each other, searching both for common themes and for differences across sectors, institutions and courses.

Case study institutions and courses

We now describe the institutions and the courses that we studied.

College A

College A was situated in a large urban catchment area, historically specialising in technical and vocational courses. In terms of the number of part-time advanced students, it was the smallest of our four case study institutions. It offered daytime, evening and mixed-mode courses. One of the courses selected had close links with one large local employer and the other course had employer links with a diverse range of organisations, both large and small.

HNC ENGINEERING

The first 'course', the HNC in Engineering, was complex since the students came from three different courses within the Engineering School: Automotive Engineering, Electrical Engineering and Engineering (Shipbuilding). All were studying for HNCs.

Automotive Engineering students were in class for two-and-a-half days per week, with a fixed timetable, and did the HNC in a year, with most of their fees funded by European Social Fund (ESF) money. It was a new course, crowded, and was, in fact, far closer to a traditional full-time course on a number of criteria: the amount of time spent in college, the amount of further studying required, the current employment status of the students and the extent of their work experience and their attitudes. The course was delivered all day Monday, all day Tuesday and half day Wednesday. The class contact time added up to just under 16 hours, presumably deliberately in order to allow students to carry on claiming Income Support. There was no overlap with other courses but the students had access to all college facilities on the same basis as full-timers. The first year of the course had five full-time students, six part-time infill students who were ESF funded and 11 evening students.

The Shipbuilding course had moved from day-release as the employer had shifted from bearing the cost of an employee being away in company time to the cheaper alternative of paying the fees. This indicates the college's responsiveness to changes in the company's timetable, offering the course on Friday afternoons when they knew that the employer's regular week finished at Friday lunchtime. The unit system provided a good deal of flexibility, with students able to vary their pace somewhat by doing two units rather than one per week if they could find enough of their own time – for example an evening a week as well as the Friday afternoon. There was some scope for credits counting towards different HNCs. The HNCs did not articulate automatically with HNDs – for instance, having done an HNC in Engineering in college A did not mean students could go on to complete an HND elsewhere (on the other hand the HNCs could count towards a degree at a local university). The employer did not encourage progression on to degrees.

The Electrical Engineering course conformed most closely to the traditional day-release pattern, with students coming to college for one full day a week. There were increasing links and overlaps between electrical and mechanical engineering programmes, marking a shift towards more generic provision.

HNC SOCIAL CARE

The second 'course' studied in college A was the HNC in Social Care. This lasted two years, scheduled regularly from 5 pm to 8 pm. It had varied in intensity, moving from one evening per week to two and back to one again. There was no overlap with other courses – the Social Care student group was virtually isolated from the rest of the student body and their access to facilities was severely limited. This was felt acutely in respect of catering and library facilities: the full-time students almost monopolised the books and a semi-private, but minimal, book stock for the class operated on an informal and not very successful basis. With the college cafeteria closed by the time they arrived, the installation of a microwave for them to make their own drinks was seen as a minimal but significant step. One student said that there was no atmosphere in the college because no one was there in the evening, although it was unclear how far this was actually the case.

Most students had a few 'O' grades only, but all had several years' experience of working in a variety of social care settings. There was no structured progression, which this may be significant in the light of employer comments about the lack of articulation between HNC and social work qualifications. Some students were thinking of studying further but, for the most part, without clear information on available opportunities. There are major questions about the professional or market currency of this HNC.

All students followed the same set of units. There was a good deal of repetition in the teaching, which reflected the fact that attendance rates are far from perfect. This was a source of frustration to some.

College B

College B was restructured following incorporation in 1994 when three smaller colleges were amalgamated, making it the largest further education provider in the locality. Subject areas were reorganised into ten sectors, each headed by managers (apparently often former teaching staff who relinquished teaching for these full-time senior administrative posts) and consisting of a number of subject-specific teams. In turn, teams are headed by (usually senior) lecturers who have responsibility for the delivery, assessment and administration of all the courses they provide. Our case study covered two HNC courses out of the 22 HNCs which are currently offered part-time. As with college A, this college offered daytime, evening and mixed-mode courses. Neither of the two selected had noticeable gender imbalances. Employer links could, perhaps, be best described as historical in the case of one, long-standing, course and tenuous, but strengthening, in the case of the other, newer course.

HNC ACCOUNTING

The first course was HNC Accounting in the Business Studies sector. This was a long-standing course with 213 part-time students in the 1995–96 intake. As with all SCOTVEC qualifications, students taking HNC Accounting required at least 12 credits and 30 credits for the HND. At college B, Accounting students were more likely to progress to professional courses and required 15 credits for exemptions from the ACCA Foundation Course. The teaching year was divided into three 12-week blocks. In Accounting, each credit typically required a weekly three-hour session (a morning, afternoon or evening) in a single block. An HNC would, therefore, require two years if studied one day per week or four years if studied one evening per week, with various combinations of evening and daytime study possible. For example, the team leader indicated that a student seeking the 15 credits for a professional exemption might be recommended to attend for one day and one evening in their first year and one day or two evenings in their second year as they can get six credits studying one day per week throughout the year and three credits studying for one evening per week. Over the period we were interviewing, units worth one, two and three credits were available. There were two core (compulsory) units offered, each worth three credits, and the remaining credits could be made up from six other optional units, all of which also count towards an HND.

A one-credit unit would be taught over one block, a two-credit unit would be taught over two blocks, and a three-credit unit would take the whole year. Due to demand, the most popular units were offered in up to three classes on up to two days and/or evenings per week. Separate daytime units were offered for part-time and full-time students, although part-timers could infill onto the full-time units. The HNC courses were periodically revalidated by SCOTVEC. The HNC Accounting was to be revalidated in the year after we conducted the study and the credit value of units as to be changed to one, one-and-a-half, and two credits to allow greater flexibility.

HNC GRAPHIC DESIGN

The second course was Graphic Design, in the Art and Design Sector. It was a smaller course with only 17 enrolments, of whom about 11 remained on the course by the end of the year. It was a newer course, having been running for about five or six years, although it had been modernised a year earlier, partly to make it more computer-oriented. It was a dedicated day-release course which students attended one day a week. The course involved a substantial amount of individual learning, with students working on briefs on their own and at their own pace. The unit structure of the course was, consequently, less apparent to students, some of whom were not sure how many credits had been available to them last year. Students wishing to progress to the HND would need to do so on an infill basis.

University C

University C was granted university status in 1992 and is situated in a large urban area. It offers a wide range of semesterised and modularised degree and postgraduate courses within three faculties, although the two programmes selected for case studies were relatively new and could be described as innovative. The first, Combined Studies, was taught mostly by infilling part-time students into full-time classes and thus largely comprised daytime courses. The other course, Health Studies, was tailored to fit the availability and academic requirements of a particular profession. Its modules were offered mostly in the evening, although a small number were available in the afternoons. This programme attracted a high proportion of female students (reflecting the high proportion of females within the profession).

COMBINED STUDIES

Combined Studies is strictly not a 'course' at all but the packaging of existing courses which allows students to accumulate enough points to qualify for a degree. It was originally available only on a part-time basis but, by the time of our study, it also allowed students to study full-time, in which case they differed from other full-time students only by not being enrolled on a named award. There were three overlapping categories of students at university C: full-timers doing named awards, part-timers doing named awards and Combined Studies students, who might be full- or part-time.

A full-time module represented four hours of teaching per week. Most part-time modules condensed this into three hours, so a Combined Studies student could be doing three- or four-hour modules and would usually be doing one or two of these per semester.

Combined Studies students were infill students. They occupied places on courses where these were available so that their acceptance into the programme did not guarantee them access to any given set of courses. The Combined Studies administrative staff were able to identify the most likely patterns of access on the basis of past experience – a combination of (low) demand and the willingness of named degree providers to accommodate Combined Studies' requests. The institution had, in one sense, moved very much towards the Combined Studies model, with modularisation and with expansion of part-time provision – a process we have called *reverse integration* (on the analogy of reverse take-overs), with the smaller agent drawing in the larger. But there was no sense of a change in the balance of power – 'infill' still connoted supplication.

Hitherto, Combined Studies had been institution-wide in the sense that the students' individual packages were made up of courses drawn from across the whole university, constrained or shaped only by guidance as to what makes up a coherent package. At the time of our study it appeared that this would be broken down into three sets of faculty-based Combined Studies, in Business Studies, Health Studies and Science and Technology, presumably with no inter-faculty packages. This blurred the distinction between named awards and Combined Studies. It posed the question of whether the move was curriculum-driven because of fears of incoherence or organisation/ budget-driven to preserve managerial tidiness.

In 1994–95 there were 73 Combined Studies students; in 1995–96, there were 61. The decline was mainly due to the efforts made by the Combined Studies staff to channel applicants, where possible, directly into named awards and because the system as a whole (nationally and institutionally) has become more flexible. In a sense, Combined Studies could be said to succeed if it disappears as a discrete entity.

HEALTH STUDIES

The second 'course', in Health Studies, was also a very complex set of awards and courses, with 700 students on the BSc programme overall. Not all of those were part-time, but it was not so much the numbers of students which made it complex as the number of awards and the permutations available. Diploma in Professional Studies in Nursing (DPSN) students were all qualified nurses and, therefore, entered with 120 points at Level One and 80 points at Level Two at a minimum. The DPSN gave them another 40 points to complete their Level Two and 80 points at Level Three, leaving them needing only another 40 points to get a degree. Most of the students (including all our interviewees) went on to take the BSc by doing further Level Three modules (and some went on to Level Four, Honours). A major initial task for the programme organiser was to draw up individual profiles for each student.

The DPSN had always been part-time. In principle it was day-release, the 'day' being 9 am to 4 pm. But this seven-hour day did not fit with the four-hour module structure. Each module comprised 48 contact hours. With an additional 127 'student effort' hours, the module totalled 175 hours – making the course cost exactly £1 per hour. Three modules per year was the standard part-time load so students did two modules in one semester and one in the other, which meant that they had a long 'day' in the first semester and a rather short one in the other.

University D

Our fourth case study institution was one of the smaller pre-1992 universities, from which we selected two General degree courses from the part-time degree programme. We looked in particular at the evening programme (EP), the largest component of the university's part-time undergraduate provision, which consisted of 16 subjects mostly from arts and social sciences. The course structure was semesterised and modularised. The Part-Time Degree Office (PTDO) arranged through the departments the provision of evening programme and summer academic programme courses, and was responsible for part-time admissions and for providing advice and information to part-time students. Departments which provided evening programme courses were funded for one additional member of staff (or equivalent), typically to act as course co-ordinator and to provide much of the tuition, although the deployment of staffing resources varied across departments. Neither of the courses we studied had noticeable gender imbalances. Both were variants of existing daytime courses for full-time students. There were few discernible employer links and advertising of the evening programme was directed towards individuals.

BUSINESS STUDIES

Under the current regulations, students studying for a General degree had to take 16 units and cover at least three subjects – between six and eight units had to be in the main subject and at least four in a second subject. Business Studies was one of 13 subjects which offered the six credits required for the main subject of the General degree (typically in a sequence of three non-advanced and three advanced courses). Each unit typically involved three hours of class time, on one evening per week, across the 12 teaching weeks of a 15-week semester. (The summer programme involved two evenings per week over six teaching weeks.) A student taking one course per semester (excluding those offered in the summer programme) would thus take eight years to complete a degree. At the time of our study two subjects offered Honours courses, which required an additional six units on top of the

16. Business Studies did not, although this was an issue under consideration. Business Studies units were provided jointly by two departments, Management & Organisation and Marketing, each of which had a course co-ordinator. There were about 50 students taking the non-advanced unit we studied.

ENGLISH STUDIES

English Studies had been one of the first departments to contribute to the evening programme but had withdrawn, and subsequently re-entered, the evening programme in 1994. Its current crop of students were consequently all in the first half of their courses. Accordingly, no students in English Studies were far enough advanced for Honours units to be made available, although it was uncertain whether English Studies would go on to offer Honours units. As with Business Studies, each unit typically involved three hours of class time, on one evening per week, over the teaching weeks of a semester. There were 12 students on the advanced unit we studied.

The organisation of part-time provision: institutional structure, strategy and change

In the rest of this chapter we review the case study courses and programmes and consider some of the issues that they illustrate concerning the organisation of part-time higher education. We first examine issues at the institutional level and then at the level of the course or programme.

In Chapter 5 we described the commitment of institutional policy makers to expanding part-time higher education and – more broadly, if more vaguely – to increasing the flexibility of provision. How were these commitments translated into the organisation of provision within the four case study institutions? In all four institutions the provision of part-time higher education needs to be seen in the context of rapid and often radical institutional change. Colleges A and B and university C had restructured in the early 1990s and we start by discussing the experience of these three institutions.

Restructuring brought three main benefits for the institutions. First, it allowed them to consolidate their competitive positions as providers in their local area – for example college B and university C amalgamated with their nearest local competitors. In the case of college B, considerable economies of scale were achieved and staffing costs were cut. Second, provision was restructured in such a way as to make it more responsive to the local labour market. In the case of college A, for example, the old organisation of the college into five divisions that served the needs of heavy industry in the locality no longer made sense. The college replaced these with nine schools and re-oriented its provision towards the needs of the growing service sector. The move towards greater HN provision in colleges A and B was at least partly explained as a response to the need for higher qualifications in the labour market. Third, provision was restructured in order to maximise flexibility, a concept which our interviewees linked with issues such as openness, access, responsiveness and diversity. As we saw in Chapter 5, most institutions were committed to increasing flexibility and to offering courses in a variety of modes. This was easiest for college B and university C, where high numbers meant that several classes on one module might be viable, but it would not have been possible without uniformity of course structure and content across modes. All three institutions had modularised their provision, making it at least technically possible for a part-time student to have access to modules from any course. College B also rearranged its timetable to facilitate part-time study; it organised daytime courses, including those which were not specifically dedicated part-time provision, in half-day teaching blocks. University C moved to a more flexible year structure by semesterising. All three institutions could thus be said to have made their full-time provision more 'part-time-friendly'.

In Chapter 5 we distinguished between two models of part-time delivery: flexible integration and flexible differentiation. The elements of institutional structure described above are typical of flexible integration – at least in principle they offer a seamless array of provision available to full- and part-time students alike in a 'part-time-friendly' manner. However, these institutions also exhibited elements of flexible differentiation in their commitment to diversity of provision and responsiveness to local labour market needs and flexible differentiation rather than flexible integration remained the dominant feature of provision in the two colleges. None of the three institutions was a pure example of either model.

These key elements of restructuring were in line with institutional policy which emphasised the institutional commitment to widening access and the importance of links with local communities, particularly local labour market needs. However, each of the case study institutions placed different emphases on these two elements of institutional policy.

In college A market research had revealed a local demand for part-time provision. There was an emphasis on the needs of the unemployed, perhaps because the majority of its provision was non-advanced and/or as a legacy of the social justice concerns of the local authority prior to incorporation. Radical restructuring of the local labour market – in particular the decline of the shipbuilding industry – had dried up supplies of students in traditional subject areas and there was a concern to meet the needs of the current labour market where the service and care sectors had become increasingly important.

A buoyant local labour market meant that college B was more concerned to meet the growing demand for qualifications. The emphasis on flexibility and openness arose out of a commitment to institutional expansion as much as to access. Senior staff expressed concern about the capping of full-time places and fluctuations in demand as a result of changes in the local economy. The college had responded to these concerns by placing greater emphasis on part-time provision and by attempting to enhance links with local employers.

In university C an enduring commitment to access throughout the institution was of prime importance. The university was one of the pioneers of SCOTCAT. However, links with employers and a commitment to vocational education were also important factors that led to greater flexibility of delivery.

These different emphases within institutional policies may be ephemeral in the context of a changing environment and they may also reflect the different perspectives of the individuals who described the policies to us. However, access and responsiveness to local labour markets underpinned the organisation of part-time higher education in all the institutions.

The fourth institution, university D, had not recently restructured, although its provision had always been modular and semesterised. It had always been theoretically possible to study part-time on an infill basis but the timetabling of the university's daytime courses (none of which were dedicated part-time courses) was not 'part-time-friendly'. Most of these courses were delivered in one-hour sessions (either a lecture or tutorial). Since there were typically three hours per week of class contact per unit, each unit might involve attendance on three separate days of the week. This would be unlikely to appeal to a part-time student, even one without other commitments.

Nevertheless, the degree structure was flexible and 'part-time-friendly' even if the timetabling of daytime courses was not. It made it possible to develop an innovative part-time degree programme, delivered in the evenings, that was equivalent or nearly equivalent to full-time courses in terms of content and assessment but which offered a narrower range of courses than was offered during the day. Moreover, university D, unlike the other three institutions, had attempted to increase flexibility by offering the summer programme where both part-time and full-time students could study semester units intensively across six weeks instead of the usual twelve.

There was no commitment by university D to flexible integration as an ideal model of provision. Indeed, a high value was placed on dedicated services for part-time and, particularly, adult students. Part-time provision was flexibly differentiated, although there was evidence of some blurring of the boundary between the full- and part-time programmes. The significance of this is further explored in the discussion of course structure below.

The development of the part-time programme arose out of a commitment to access and a concern for the needs of adult students. Particularly important was the development and growth of a division charged with innovation in educational practice and which acted as a 'single door' for adult entrants. Funding provided by the SHEFC's Flexbility In Teaching and Learning Scheme was an important factor in getting the programme off the ground, although the programme began in advance of this funding.

In conclusion, institutional structure and strategy were important in creating the conditions necessary for the development and expansion of part-time provision. The commitment to increase flexibility of provision throughout the institution was a particularly significant factor in college A, college B and university C. Nevertheless, we find evidence both of flexible integration (greatest in university C) and of flexible differentiation (more pronounced in colleges A and B and in university D). Modularisation and credit transfer were important elements in both aspects of flexibility but it may be useful to distinguish between flexibility in respect of qualifications and course structures and flexibility in respect of timetabling and delivery which is necessary for flexible integration.

The organisation of part-time provision: degree courses
DIVERSITY OF PART-TIME COURSES

We now turn our attention to the organisation of part-time provision at the level of the course or programme, although this is a difference of focus more than of content. Many of our themes – especially flexibility – are the same as we identified at the institutional level. The eight courses chosen for study illustrate the diversity of part-time provision. They also show how arbitrary it can be to define a discrete part-time 'course'. One of the courses (Engineering in college A) divided into a variety of specialist strands. Within university C, one of the courses studied (Health Studies) was a complex network of provision with exit points at several different qualification levels, the other (Combined Studies) embraced a huge variety of curricular combinations and drew on provision from across the university. In university D the two courses we studied were subject strands within the same degree programme, in which all students selected units from different strands. In the following discussion we reduce a little of this complexity by looking first at degree-level courses and then at HNCs.

SEGREGATED AND INTEGRATED MODELS OF PROVISION

University D came nearest to an example of *segregated* or dedicated part-time provision. Several factors discouraged the integration of part-time and full-time study. These included the timetable (with daytime delivery based on one-hour sessions), the attitudes of staff and the traditional research focus of the university, all of which would have impeded the culture change required to make the daytime provision more part-time-friendly. While there was no policy to increase part-time participation on daytime courses, barriers to integration in the other direction (full-time students participating in the part-time programme) had recently been removed. New regulations allowed full-time students to study all three units per semester in the evening, although part-time students still had priority for places in the evening. The summer programme had proved equally attractive to full-time and part-time students. Much as the Combined Studies degree in university C helped to promote flexibility across the institution as a whole, the evening programme in university D opened up the potential for full-time students to participate in a more flexible manner. But the programme saw itself as offering something over and above 'normal' provision, rather than as promoting a transformation of the institution as a whole. For example, some of the units available in the evening programme were not available during the day. University D's segregated model offered specific benefits such as dedicated services and guidance for part-time students, a 'single door' for adult entrants including continuity of support from access to degree study and flexibility in admissions procedures. Teaching methods in the two subjects we studied appeared more flexible in the evening programme than on daytime courses – they allowed for greater student participation, and deadlines and attendance requirements were applied less strictly.

But segregated provision had its down side. At university D it reduced the flexibility of provision for part-time students. Options were restricted. The higher costs of dedicated and, therefore, smaller, part-time classes meant that a much smaller number of courses was offered than for full-time programmes and it was harder to provide teaching across all specialisms. Honours provision was particularly problematic. The trade-off between choice and cost is less favourable in a segregated model. These problems were aggravated, in some cases, by the resistance of staff to teaching on the part-time programme. Choice and flexibility were further restricted by timetabling considerations, with only four evening slots per semester.

Combined Studies at university C was the clearest example of *integrated* provision and provides a useful contrast. It involved a similar number of class contact hours per module but the time of day depended on the options chosen by the student. The flexibility of this programme depended on the availability of places and the willingness of departments to accommodate part-time students. Part-time students' choices were also constrained by the restrictions of a timetable designed for full-time students.

CATs was important in enabling students to study part-time in university C, particularly in the Health Studies programme, because it reduced the total time required to achieve a degree. Of our 11 interviewees at university C, only one was taking more than four years to complete her degree on a part-time basis. The downside to this is that the combination of modularisation and CATs makes progression from one award to another easier, weakening the rationale for sticking to a lower award and increasing the pressure towards credential inflation. This might reduce the currency of hard-won qualifications.

Within university C the integrated provision of Combined Studies contrasted with the dedicated provision on the Health Studies course. While Combined Studies was wholly integrated, it remained marginal, although modularisation reduced its marginal status. Options depended on the availability of infill places for full-time as well as part-time and Combined Studies students felt isolated and not part of the mainstream. The move to faculty-based Combined Studies degrees might, however, resolve the problems of marginality and the difficulty of negotiating places for students. This underlines the need to investigate critically the apparent flexibility of provision in practice.

Health Studies, on the other hand, was dedicated provision designed specifically for part-time students and this increased the flexibility of the programme in terms of the timing of delivery (modules were repeated during the week and students could opt to attend on different evenings as it suited them) and the choice of subjects available. Health studies in university C contrasts with the part-time degree programme at university D. Each programme had a similar number of students (approximately 600 students in Health Studies), they were spread over a wider range of subjects in university D and this restricted the options which were available. Size matters, and a higher number of students increases choice and flexibility.

RESOURCES AND STAFFING

All the part-time degree programmes had considerable administrative and resource implications. A major task in the Health Studies programme in university C was the drawing up of individual student profiles and study paths by academic staff. A similar exercise was undertaken in respect of Combined Studies by the Centre for Continuing Education. In addition, as Combined Studies students 'infilled' onto other programmes, course choice was limited by places available and the Centre's staff had the task of negotiating places with faculties and course leaders. There are parallels here with university D, which also had dedicated administrative support for part-time students in the shape of the Part-Time Degree Office (PTDO). This organised classes, registered students and offered advice and information to part-time students. It was located in a division whose remit included 'access' and innovation in educational practice.

Academic staff there offered pre-entry interviews on course advice and learning support to part-time students.

The provision of dedicated information and support services could lead to tension between those providing these services and the staff providing the courses which part-time students wished to study. At university C some course leaders were more sympathetic than others to requests for places for Combined Studies students. Similarly, at university D we were aware of tensions between the PTDO and departments over the 'ownership' of part-time students.

Most staff in university C were used to teaching in a variety of modes but evening teaching had been a new departure for most staff in university D. We found a wide range of attitudes and commitment to part-time teaching among staff members, with a small number of enthusiasts and a large number of non-involved staff. The non-involvement of the majority may have simply been a consequence of the allocation of teaching responsibilities, given that the part-time degree programme funded only one member of teaching staff per department. However, some staff were concerned about the implications of evening teaching for their conditions of employment, while others were unwilling to divert their efforts from research, given time pressures. Such concerns may have influenced the decision by some departments not to participate in the programme. Nevertheless, a majority of the departments in the Arts and Human Sciences Schools were involved in the evening programme and this was made possible by the additional resources available in terms of staffing.

The fact that the evening programme was taught by relatively few people had several consequences. It was difficult to offer higher level and, especially, Honours courses which required inputs from specialist staff – course co-ordinators often did much of the teaching themselves and heads of participating departments felt obliged to teach. There was a lack of ownership of the evening programme by departments, aggravated by the role of the PTDO as the main point of communication with students. When students were released by departments into the modularised curriculum there were implications for the internal allocation of resources, the co-ordination of provision and for student support and guidance. Therefore, considerable staffing resources were required for the management and administration of the programmes and guidance of students in both universities in the shape of the PTDO and dedicated non-teaching Combined Studies staff.

None of the degree-level courses had strong links with employers. This was particularly surprising in the case of Health Studies since it represented a large set of programmes driven by external changes in the professional division of labour and qualification requirements. While Health Studies is driven by the need to respond to professional changes, the others could be said to be driven by an institutional commitment to widen access to higher education and so the lack of employer links was, perhaps, less surprising.

The organisation of part-time provision: HNC courses
RESPONSIVENESS TO LABOUR MARKETS
AND MODELS OF FLEXIBLE DELIVERY

The Engineering HNCs at college A were offered in a variety of modes that were conditioned by external factors. Only the Automotive strand had no links with employers. Of the three groups of students studying the course, the part-time infill students were, perhaps, the most interesting because while this group was studying part-time, they would complete the course in one rather than two years. These students were unemployed and the ESF had funded 16 hours of class contact time which allowed them to study the course at a full-time pace but retain the status of part-time students, according to Department of Social Security (DSS) regulations which governed the payment of their income support. The course was delivered during the day over two-and-a-half days per week. Therefore, the provision of ESF funding made the provision of places to unemployed students viable and the number of hours of contact was at least partly conditioned by DSS regulations.

There were strong and long-standing links with the local shipbuilding industry. Provision had originally been on a day-release basis but this changed to full-time when the traditional demand from the industry dried up. This was changed again when full-time places were capped and modules were offered on evenings and Friday afternoons as well as on a traditional day-release basis. The move to evenings and Friday afternoons was a response to the employer's desire to move away from the expensive day-release mode. By attending on more than one evening, students were able to vary their pace of studying.

The HNC in Social Care at college A was a new course and there were, therefore, no long-standing relationships with employers. The development of the course was a response to the growth of the care sector where staff are poorly qualified. Relationships with employers were developed when college staff arranged placements for full-time students. Employers showed an interest in HNC provision for their own staff and the college decided to develop a part-time strand delivered in the evenings. Chronic under-funding and low levels of staffing in the care sector made day-release unrealistic. However, at the time of our study college staff worried whether employer interest would be maintained in the wake of local government reorganisation – the willingness to pay fees was already patchy.

The diversity of modes of delivery and relationships with the labour market in college A illustrate very well the model of flexible differentiation. The need to respond quickly to segmented markets, the constraints of funding, the restructuring of the labour market, changes in employer demand and the constraints of DSS regulations all had a bearing on the decision to offer courses in particular modes. These changes cannot be glossed over simply as increasing student choice. The reality is more complex and tells us as much about constraints as choices.

In college B, although provision was dedicated, it was formally open to all students and so there was formal integration, particularly as day-time provision was timetabled in a part-time-friendly manner. The scale of the institution and its monopoly as a provider in the local area meant that it was possible to offer the same units in a variety of modes simultaneously and so students could combine different modes, which increased the flexibility for full-time as well as part-time students. Both the size of the institution and the standardised nature of HNC units meant that options were not restricted for part-time students.

HNC Accounting was a good example of dedicated provision with formal integration, which provides for flexibility on the margins. All provision is open to all students but part-time HNC Accounting students have separate timetables. The opportunity to take a mixture of part-time daytime and evening units allowed part-time day students to infill on part-time evening classes and vice versa. This allowed the college to meet the needs of a segmented market consisting of both large and small employers, not all of whom would be able to release staff during the day. In contrast, student numbers on the HNC Graphic Design were too small to allow a range of modes of delivery and this course was offered only by day-release. The college had recently set up formal links with employers in the shape of liaison committees (see Chapter 9) but it remains to be seen how or if this will affect the nature of provision.

Another aspect of flexibility was the extent to which the HNCs articulated with other courses and thereby provided flexible opportunities for progression. Here there was significant variation between the colleges and across courses. At college B both HNCs articulated with HNDs offered by the college, although the HND in Graphic Design had no dedicated part-time strand so part-time students would have to study on an infill basis. The more usual progression route from the HNC Accounting was into a professional award, for which the HNC would contribute credit. At college A there was no employer support for progression from Engineering HNCs to HNDs and the college was unable to offer it. Nor was there any structured progression from the HNC in Social Care, which appeared to have a doubtful professional/market currency and which had no relationship with other social work qualifications. Given that only the day-release Engineering at college A appeared to offer a clear chance of career improvement, our findings raise questions about the currency of the HNC.

RESOURCES AND STAFFING

Neither of the colleges had dedicated administrative services for part-time students similar to those in the universities, presumably because the majority of students in both institutions were part-time rather than full-time. Of course, this does not mean that part-time students might not have benefited from dedicated services, as we see in Chapter 8 below. For example, in college A full-time students on the HNC Social Care always got to the library books first. This led to the setting up of a small private library for part-time students.

There were differences between the two colleges in staff conditions. In college A staff were paid for teaching in the evening, although some staff recognised that this might be about to change. Staff did not welcome this prospect and drew attention to the increases in their workload in recent years, particularly the increases in assessment load. One commented that the changes would not only affect hours and pay arrangements but would also require a culture change for college staff who were unused to operating in a competitive market.

College A operated in a highly competitive local environment and this increased staff's feelings of insecurity. Staff who were interviewed invariably referred to the activities of other institutions and were aware that they might be competing for the same students. It is possible that increased competition had intensified workloads. The HNC in Social Care appeared to be severely under-staffed, although the course leader was hopeful that they would be allocated additional staff in the near future. The part-time strand of this course relied heavily on one part-time member of staff employed on a short-term contract basis who combined this with similar contract work at other further education institutions in the area. As this member of staff was paid by the piece during term time and without security of employment, he was obliged to work very long hours. An important dimension of the flexibility of provision in this case, therefore, was the ability to draw on a flexible source of teaching labour.

In college B staff were given time off in lieu of evening teaching but not paid. There was a recognition in the college of the need for greater flexibility in staffing and an explicit policy to employ 12–15 per cent of staff on a part-time basis. The Art & Design Sector had tried to increase flexibility in the deployment of staff by introducing team teaching and, as a result, staff taught over a wider range of subjects. There was no sense of resistance to evening teaching on the part of staff, the majority of whom taught in the evenings.

Conclusion

The commitment to increase flexibility was a significant factor in all of the institutions studied and, especially, in the two colleges and in university C. This commitment could reflect different goals or emphases – for instance, some institutions gave more priority to access and others to responsiveness to local labour markets. Moreover, the shared commitment to flexibility translated into a variety of ways of organising part-time provision. Some of this variety is expressed in terms of the distinction, introduced in Chapter 5, between flexible integration and flexible differentiation. There was a stronger emphasis on flexible integration in university C and more emphasis on flexible differentiation in colleges A and B and in university D, but in each institution there was a distinctive blend incorporating elements of both models and there was further variation between courses within each institution.

However, the organisation of part-time provision varied in further ways. Integrated provision – available to full-time and part-time students alike – could be more or less 'part-time-friendly' depending on such factors as the timetabling of courses, the conditions of access to courses, the attitudes of staff and the nature of supporting services. Dedicated part-time provision was organised very differently in institutions where it was part of mainstream provision than in those, such as university D, where it consciously differed from that mainstream. Institutions and courses differed in the way they staffed part-time courses and in the location of ownership of part-time provision. The local labour market, and links with employers, were further influences on the organisation of part-time provision and will be examined in detail in Chapter 9.

Chapter 7

Part-Time Students in the Four Institutions

Social and demographic characteristics

We interviewed 43 students individually (in addition to those who took part in group discussions), all of whom were studying on one of the eight courses. The survey covered 556 students from a wide range of part-time undergraduate courses in the four institutions and in the OU. In this chapter we present the social and educational backgrounds of these students, their demographic characteristics and their motives for studying.

More than half (25 out of 43) of the students whom we interviewed were female and 38 were in full-time jobs (the other five were unemployed). Their ages ranged from 19 to 61 and the median student was in his or her thirties. However, our interviewees were not necessarily representative of all part-time students – they were not selected systematically and their availability and willingness to be interviewed may well have depended upon their attitude to the course, their employment status or other personal characteristics. The survey sample was designed to be representative of all part-time undergraduate students at the four case study institutions, together with the OU. Table 7.1 summarises their social and demographic characteristics, broken down by sector.

There was an equal gender split among the sample as a whole. The proportion of females was highest in the two (non-Open) universities (60%) and lowest in the colleges (37%), with the OU in between (48%). In this respect our sample reflected the national trend – across Scotland, females constitute a higher proportion of part-time undergraduate entrants in higher education institutions than in further education colleges (55% compared with 42% in 1994–95: Scottish Office 1996, p.7). College students were more likely to attend courses during the day and this may help to explain the gender difference between sectors. Females comprised a higher proportion of students who attended in the evenings only (57%) than of students who attended during the day (44%) or by other modes, which included distance learning (47%).

There was a wide age range among students. As with the interviewees, the median student was in his or her thirties but the age distribution varied across the sectors – half the college students (50%) were aged 30 or less, compared with 37 per cent of university students and about a quarter (26%) of OU students. Once again, the sector difference partly reflected mode of attendance – 58 per cent of day students were aged 30 or less, compared with 30 per cent of evening students and 26 per cent of other modes. The age distributions of male and female students were similar.

About four in ten students had children whom they described as 'dependent on [them] for care or financial support'. The highest proportion was among the OU students (48%). Slightly more males than females had dependent children, suggesting that women with dependants were more likely to be deterred from studying, but the difference was small (42% against 36%). Some students had no dependent children but said that a partner (5%) or other adult (3%) was dependent on them.

Three-quarters of all students were in full-time jobs. By sector, the largest proportion was among college students (86%) and all the college students were economically active – that is, in a full- or part-time job or unemployed and seeking work. The OU had the lowest proportion of students in full-time jobs (61%) and had a considerable minority of economically inactive students, most of them home-makers or retired.

Students were asked to describe their present or most recent job. Overall, nearly a third (32%) were in 'associate professional and technical' occupations, a category which included technicians, nurses and welfare workers. There was a strong contrast between sectors – university students were the most likely to be in 'associate professional and technical' occupations (48%), while a majority of college students were either in 'clerical and secretarial' occupations (24%) or in 'craft and related' occupations (29%). The occupational distribution differed predictably between males and females.

The case studies allow us to put flesh on these demographic statistics by showing how part-time study fitted into students' individual biographies and their changing circumstances. The students we interviewed included young employees with no dependants who were ambitious for their careers or who were sent by

Table 7.1 Characteristics of sample members (percentages)

	Colleges	Universities	OU	All
Gender				
Male	63	40	52	50
Female	37	60	48	50
Age				
Up to 30 years	50	37	26	37
31–40 years	32	35	44	37
Over 40 years	18	28	30	26
Dependants				
Dependant children	33	36	48	39
Dependent adult, no children	6	2	2	3
Dependent partner	4	4	6	5
No dependants	57	58	44	54
Labour-market status				
Full-time paid job	86	78	61	75
Part-time paid job	6	11	10	9
Unemployed and looking for work	7	3	6	5
Unable to work (e.g. disabled)	0	1	2	1
Full-time unpaid work at home	0	2	8	4
Retired	0	2	8	3
Other	1	2	5	3
Present or most recent occupation				
Management, admin and professional	20	27	18	23
Associate professional and technical	13	48	26	32
Clerical and secretarial	24	13	17	17
Craft and related	29	4	8	12
Others	14	8	31	16
Sample n (=100%)	*145*	*243*	*168*	*556*

their employers; young-to-middle-aged employees, many with dependents, who wanted to develop personally and/or professionally, often because their careers had seemed to plateau out and they were becoming bored; middle-aged or older employees who wished to protect their position in an insecure labour market and against competition from younger and better-qualified entrants; people in part-time or intermittent employment, who had more time to study and who wished to consolidate their experience and qualifications to support a return to the full-time labour market; the unemployed, whose motives were similar but who typically had less work experience to consolidate and for whom the choice of a specific career path was often more arbitrary; adults with more time on their hands, typically as a result of their children becoming more independent or leaving home; and adults approaching retirement or semi-retirement.

We discuss personal and vocational motives for study in more detail below. The categories of student described above are neither exhaustive nor exclusive. Our case studies reveal the diversity and complexity of the biographical factors which lay behind students' participation. Part-time study was often the outcome of a complex interaction of occupational, personal and domestic circumstances. To take just one example, a student at university C was not currently able to work full-time because she was caring for a very elderly and frail grandparent. Part-time study complemented her caring role by providing a challenging way of using the gaps in her timetable and by helping her to prepare for a return to full-time employment.

Educational backgrounds

In Chapters 1 and 2 we suggested that public debates about higher education have been premised on a notion of the typical student who was young, had recently left school, had not yet entered the full-time labour market and who studied full-time. As Table 7.1 shows, most part-time students diverge from this norm in respect of age and employment as well as mode of study. The educational background of the 'typical' full-time student is that of a first-time entrant, with Highers or A level qualifications from school, who has not entered any other post-school courses. Once again, part-time students differ markedly from this pattern.

In the first place, a large proportion of all part-time students – more than four in ten of our sample – had already obtained higher education qualifications or part-qualifications. The first panel of Table 7.2 shows that the highest proportion was among university students, of whom 52 per cent reported higher education qualifications. The second panel shows that these tended to be nursing qualifications, HNC/Ds or other higher education certificates or diplomas, although 10 per cent of university students reported that they had a degree. A significant minority of college and OU students said they had higher education qualifications, most often an HNC/D. It is possible that higher education qualifications were over-reported if some students reported either the qualification to which they were currently working or credits already received towards it. This may account for many of the college students who reported higher education qualifications. Among our interviewees – whose accounts we could check against this misinterpretation – one college student and ten (out of 21) university students had previously been in higher education, including two who had not completed their earlier courses but were using credits from them towards current courses.

Second, among those who had not previously been in higher education, a majority of college students and a significant minority of university students had left school without achieving Highers or equivalent academic qualifications for entry to higher education. In this respect, part-time education appears to have fulfilled its conventionally ascribed role of offering a 'second chance' for early school leavers.

Third, the vast majority of our interviewees (38 out of 43) and of sample members (88%) had already gained qualifications since leaving school and many had gained several qualifications. Our interview data enabled us to examine the links between this prior experience and their current course. In nearly all cases their current courses built on these earlier qualifications, sometimes in terms of vertical progression but often through a sideways move to a related field – for example from nursing to psychology. Many students received credit recognition for their earlier qualifications, especially in university C, where this was an important feature of the Combined Studies course. More than half the survey sample had studied on a previous part-time course.

Our data suggest that the rhetoric of 'second chance' education may no longer be adequate to describe part-time higher education in Scotland in the 1990s. The notion of 'second chance' education tends

Table 7.2 Educational backgrounds of sample members (percentages)

	Colleges	Universities	OU	All
Level of academic attainment	43	19	33	30
No Higher or A levels from school	28	29	32	30
School Highers or A levels	28	29	32	30
HE qualifications	29	52	35	41
Post-school qualifications (multiple responses possible)				
Academic qualification below HE	17	29	26	25
Vocational qualification below HE	72	41	54	53
Craft or technician apprenticeship	31	5	12	14
Nursing qualification	0	27	8	14
HNC or HND	21	24	23	23
Other HE certificate or diploma	6	23	10	14
Degree	6	10	5	8
Other qualification				
Any post-school qualification	90	90	83	88
Whether/when studied part-time				
Yes, since 1990	39	29	30	32
1981–90	15	13	16	14
Before 1981	11	4	9	7
Never	36	54	45	47
Sample n (=100%)	145	243	168	556

to assume that higher education is the main form of post-school learning, that it is a discrete, undifferentiated and one-off experience, and that normal access to higher education is via a single, school-based route. But our study shows that many students have gained other (non-higher education) qualifications since leaving school, that there is considerable scope for progression (vertical or horizontal) between levels and types of undergraduate higher education and that access to higher education via other post-school courses is a 'normal' avenue of advancement for many adults, many of whom left school without entry qualifications to higher education. The rhetoric of 'second chance' education ignores the diversity of part-time higher education and the extent to which different educational episodes, both at higher education level and below, may be progressive and cumulative experiences.

Teaching staff's perceptions of part-time students

Staff in all four institutions said that part-time students were more committed and motivated, took their studies more seriously and were more rewarding to teach. Many students contrasted their own more serious approach with that of their children or of themselves when previously full-time students. Some part-time students who attended courses alongside full-time students commented on the different student culture and many felt that the full-timers were less motivated and had less favourable attitudes. Students on largely dedicated part-time courses, as at university D, tended to appreciate the fact that their fellow students had similar circumstances and motivations – many of them would not have welcomed greater mixing of full- and part-time students. However, several interviewees stressed that full- and part-timers alike varied widely in their motivation and attitudes. One staff member felt that the cliché that part-timers were more strongly committed was a slur on full-time students, many of whom were strongly motivated and many of whom were adults. And some part-time students commented that the financial difficulties and the difficult labour market made the current situation of full-time students more serious than that of earlier generations – their own position was ultimately easier because they had alternative statuses (for example employee, member of family or household) and a secure income stream to fall back on.

Some interviewees felt that the different commitment and motivation of full- and part-time students reflected differences in age and maturity; part-timers had already sown their wild oats and had a clearer and more focused purpose for studying. Others felt that the circumstances of part-time study also contributed to the difference. Most part-time students had paid for their courses, or their employers had paid on their behalf, and they felt an obligation to work hard to justify the expenditure. Most part-time students, especially evening students, had further demonstrated their commitment in terms of the substantial time devoted to their studies.

Many staff felt that part-time students were more demanding. They were more mature and could better articulate their demands and expectations. They often had more experience of the subject under study and were less easily satisfied if (for example) the course was out of date or did not correspond to their own workplace experience. They were more likely to have domestic or work commitments and therefore valued their own time highly. They were more likely to resent classes, particularly if little effort had been made to notify them. Several staff commented on the 'customer culture' of part-time students, who had higher expectations and felt that deadlines and attendance requirements should not apply to them. A staff member in university D commented: 'They feel that because they've paid their money it's their right to come and go as they wish. ...If you've paid money for a course it does put you in a different relationship ... that's part of the creation of a different kind of culture about education that's inherent in the whole project.' The customer culture was reflected in the comments of several of the students. For example, some students perceived that part-timers were being 'short-changed' and that the resources they attracted were not being fed back into part-time provision or facilities.

Staff were reluctant to generalise about part-time students but they mentioned other characteristics of part-time students which had implications for their educational needs. These included:

- their initial anxiety, especially among those who had had a substantial break from learning, about their ability to study and to handle assignments (university D encouraged new students to attend study skills courses, which were highly regarded by the students we spoke to)

- their greater experience, for example of the 'practical' aspects of many vocational courses, which might require a different approach from full-time courses for young students with no workplace experience

- a greater willingness to participate in classes

- less time for study and, especially, to read outside the immediate subject of the course, which required a more 'packaged' approach

- more specific guidance needs – part-time students often have a clearer view than full-timers of where they want to go and 'need advice on how to get there rather than on where to go.' (acting course leader, college B)

Table 7.3 'What were your reasons for starting your course of study? – tick all that apply' (percentages)

Reason	Colleges	Universities	OU	All
It is an opportunity to gain an educational qualification	61	63	71	65
Vocational :				
It was required in my job	24	9	0	10
To help me get on in my present job	54	46	17	40
To improve my chances in the job market	80	54	62	63
Personal:				
Because of my interest in a particular subject	43	47	61	51
It is an opportunity to develop generally	49	67	70	64
It is something constructive to do	27	35	52	38
For social contact	4	9	6	7
Another reason	1	10	9	8
Sample n (=100%)	*145*	*243*	*168*	*556*

Reasons for part-time study

Sample members were given a list of possible reasons for starting their courses and asked to tick all those that applied to them. Their answers are given in Table 7.3. A majority in each sector said that the opportunity to gain a qualification was a reason for studying, although this in itself does not tell us why the qualification was itself desired. The next three items in the list are the most directly 'vocational' and drew the highest responses from college students, although a majority of students in each sector said they studied 'to improve my chances in the job market'. Compared with other university students, OU students were less likely to study to advance themselves in their current job and more likely to do so in order to improve their chances in the job market. The next three items refer to the more 'personal' or intrinsic benefits of study – they attracted the highest response from OU students and the lowest from college students.

The difference between sectors is confirmed by a further question, which invited respondents to underline the 'most important' reason (not shown in table). Almost three quarters (74%) of college students underlined one of the 'vocational' reasons, compared with less than half (43%) of university students and little more than a third (35%) of OU students. Conversely, 15 per cent of college students, 36 per cent

Table 7.4 Combination of reasons for study (percentages)

Reason	*Colleges*	*Universities*	*OU*	*All*
Vocational and personal	72	56	61	62
Vocational only	24	18	7	16
Personal only	3	25	30	21
Neither	6	1	2	2
Sample n (=100%)	*145*	*243*	*168*	*556*

of university students and 43 per cent of OU students underlined one of the 'personal' reasons.

Most students combined 'vocational' and 'personal' reasons (Table 7.4). Nearly three-quarters of college students (72%), and a majority of students in the other two sectors, reported at least one 'vocational' reason and at least one 'personal' reason for study. There was some variation across sectors but in each sector a majority of students reported both 'vocational' and 'personal' reasons. There was similar variation across modes of study, with the day students most likely to report only 'vocational' reasons but more than 60 per cent of students in each mode gave both types of reasons. Older students (in their 40s or later) were more likely to study for purely 'personal' reasons (42%).

This overlap of vocational and personal motives was confirmed by our interviews with students on the case-study courses. These cast further light on the 'vocational' motives of part-time students.

First, in areas or fields where job prospects were uncertain, part-time study was often a defensive strategy. A Shipbuilding student explained: 'I've just been transferred to the Goods Inwards department from the Machine Shop. At the back of my mind is the thought that if they can do without me in the Machine Shop they might do without me in the Goods Inwards also'. A qualification would make him more competitive on the internal labour market as well as the external one. Several Social Care students at college A, and Health Studies students at university C, wanted higher qualifications to protect themselves against competition from younger and better-qualified people entering the profession. Even where students did not feel their jobs were under threat – as was the case for most students at university D – they often felt that the competition from better-qualified entrants made further qualifications necessary to keep promotion prospects open.

Second, across all four institutions the perceived vocational returns to part-time study were often generalised, long-term and uncertain. Most students hoped for some occupational advantage from their studies, either with their current employer or through a change of job, but they rarely knew precisely how, or when, this would occur. It is, perhaps, not surprising that they often sought personal returns from their courses as well, as these might be more predictable than specifically vocational returns:

Elisabeth is 28 and single. She attends university one evening a week. She is a staff midwife and currently pays her own fees for Health

Studies but may in future get a contribution towards them from her employer. She requested time off to do assignments and may use her holiday entitlement for study. She started studying to keep in the running for promotion because so many other nurses have qualifications. Elisabeth feels she has been pushed into studying by her employer as qualifications are necessary for promotion – more and more colleagues are studying. The most significant advantage of studying is that she fancies the idea of having a degree and will be proud of her achievement. She can afford to pay the fees as she is working. The biggest disadvantage is that she can't afford to furnish her flat as well and she finds the university's fees expensive. She also wonders if, in the long run, the degree will be of much benefit as so many other nurses are getting qualifications too. Overall, she's enjoying studying now and she didn't think she ever would. It broadens her horizons, makes her think more about her job and she finds she's able to keep up more with new technology. 'When you see some older nurses who are resistant to changing practices, you realise how necessary study is.'

Third, many students felt bored or insufficiently stretched in their jobs. Part-time study could simultaneously provide a personal challenge and stimulation, and an opportunity to increase their personal fulfilment and sense of professionalism within their current jobs. If it eventually led to promotion or a better job as well, that would be an added bonus. For example, some Business Studies students at university D welcomed the opportunity to study the changing context of their administrative jobs. Many Social Care students at college A were motivated by a sense of professionalism – they felt they were making good their employers' failure to provide the training required to maintain high professional standards of care. This mixture of personal challenge, job enrichment and career advancement was present, in varying proportions, in the motives of many of the students we spoke to. It is well illustrated by the experience of one of the Social Care students:

> Lydia chose to do the course because there was no training in the workplace and the level of practice is poor. It was important to her to set high standards of professional practice. She felt that she would be stuck in a position where standards were low and be unable to move elsewhere unless she improved her own training and gained a qualification. She had been disappointed that she had not so far received promotion and hoped for a management position.

While these factors had influenced her decision to study the course, later on the personal satisfaction she felt in completing written work was an important factor in sustaining motivation.

This example illustrates a fourth point: that motivations may change over time. Other students also reported that they had increasingly appreciated the more intrinsic or personal benefits of study.

Other influences

There were other influences on the decision to study. Partly due to its modular and semesterised structure, the part-time programme at university D provided flexibility in respect of pacing and credit transfer (in and out) as well as choice of units. This flexibility was appreciated by the students, especially those who wished to accelerate their coverage of the programme, but was not a major influence on their decision to participate. Many students were unaware of the flexibility of the course before joining. At university C, by contrast, the credit recognition offered by the Combined Studies course was an important incentive to participate. Several students were using it to upgrade existing qualifications, gain credit from courses from which they had dropped out or move sideways.

Students who were paying their own fees identified the cost of study as a disadvantage. Some suggested ways in which the burden might be eased. For example, students might be allowed to pay in instalments rather than through a single up-front payment as was required in some of the institutions studied. (Staff pointed out that the current arrangement gave the institution a financial advantage as it benefited from dropout.) However, the general feeling among many of the students we talked to was that fees were less important than the time commitment in deciding whether or not to enrol. It must be remembered, of course, that we were talking to students who had decided to study notwithstanding the fees.

One in seven (14%) of survey students said that they had applied, or seriously considered applying, to a different institution. The proportion was highest among university students (21%) and lowest among college students (7%). Most students said that they had received information about their chosen course and institution from the institution itself. Other sources of information included employers (mentioned by nearly a quarter of college students), friends or relatives (mentioned by nearly a quarter of university students) and advertisements. Our interviews suggested that information gained by word of mouth was more influential as it could recommend courses to potential students, rather than simply inform them. One student at university D told us that his line manager had been encouraged by his example to enrol on the course.

Conclusion

Like other studies, our research reveals the enormous diversity of part-time higher education students, and of their backgrounds, circumstances and aspirations. There is no 'typical' part-time higher education student. Future policy and provision for part-time higher education and for lifelong learning must recognise and accommodate this diversity. However, part-time students share some common characteristics. Except in the OU, nearly all were economically active and most were in full-time jobs. University students most commonly had technician-level jobs and college students more often had clerical or craft occupations. Part-time students were generally perceived to be more highly motivated than full-time students, to be more demanding to teach and to exhibit a 'customer culture'.

Part-time higher education was typically a further step in a post-school educational career. Most students had already gained qualifications since school, often by part-time study, and their current courses usually built on their previous qualifications in one way or another. The rhetoric of part-time higher education as 'second chance' education no longer reflects current circumstances. It ignores the enormous diversity of part-time higher education, neglects the variety and extent of post-school learning, and disregards the extent to which different educational experiences may be cumulative and progressive. The rhetoric needs to be replaced by a notion of part-time higher education as a 'further step', which may be larger or smaller, upwards or sideways.

The courses we studied illustrate the importance of broader 'generic' skills for both economic and personal development. In this respect, our study is consistent with much recent educational debate. But it also suggests that as generic skills become more important, we need to modify traditional ways of thinking about demand and the market for higher education. One implication is that as concepts of skills become less precise, the market becomes harder to interpret.

Most students entering part-time higher education expected some occupational returns but these were typically non-specific, long-term and uncertain. Many entered courses to defend existing jobs rather than to promote career development – some as a more desperate response to unemployment. We need to move beyond simplistic notions such as 'learning pays'.

Vocational and personal motives for study were closely intertwined. Generic skills are, by definition, as relevant to personal development and growth as they are to career advancement and, for many of our students, these two goals coincided. Others started with more specific occupational goals but came to appreciate the value of learning in terms of personal growth or came to seek job enrichment as much as career advancement. Given the uncertain occupational rewards, it is not surprising that, for many students, personal motives were at least as important as occupational ones in their motives for study. An institution's marketing strategy – or a nation's higher education policy – will fail if it ignores this duality.

We conclude by contrasting two of our students, whose cases encapsulate much of the diversity of part-time study:

> Stewart is an engineering student at college A, attending one day a week. He is 22 and lives with his parents, who are very supportive of him doing the course, as are his colleagues at work. His employer pointed him towards the course and is paying his fees. Although he is well satisfied with the course and feels that he is learning more advanced things than at his workplace, he does not think of himself as a student – the course is part of his employment and he is there for a specific purpose. Stewart represents, in most respects, the traditional day-release clientele and the course is, for him, the first rung on a career ladder.

> By contrast, Brenda is a teacher in a private primary school, aged 61 with grown-up children. She is studying English at university D, chiefly to prove to herself that she can do it and to complete an academic record which was never quite established. The course work does help her in her teaching but her headmaster is not very interested – although her peers in the school are impressed with the fact that she is doing the course. It has enlarged her intellectual and social horizons and should stand her in good stead when she comes to retire, but it is also allowing her to round off a professional career by gaining an appropriate qualification.

Chapter 8

The Student Experience

In this chapter we look at the experience of being a student, combining survey data with more qualitative information from the case study interviews. We cover students' perceptions of the quality of their course and of the institution generally. We look in more detail at some aspects of this, including the relationship between study and work. And we deal with student perceptions of the costs and benefits of studying, both in the present and those anticipated. Quantitative analysis centres round a small number of key variables: educational sector, gender, age and occupational position; the qualitative information is naturally more diverse.

Course quality perceptions

Part-time/full-time

First, we asked a general question in our survey about whether students felt that in their institution the quality of provision was better for part-timers or for full-timers. Significantly, 168 (30%) did not answer this and almost as many (161) responded by saying that they did not know. Of the 214 that did answer, just over half (109) felt that there was no difference. But of those who did feel that there was a difference, almost all (95 out of 105) felt that full-timers were better provided for. This was especially the case in the university sector, where 30 per cent of all respondents felt that provision was better for full-timers. In the college sector only 18 per cent felt this, but over half of those who responded said they did not know. In both cases only tiny numbers – 2 per cent and 3 per cent respectively – felt that provision for part-timers was better. How far this is a matter of the grass being greener on the other side is hard to judge, but the split is heavily weighted in one direction.

So how far are the experiences we report those of part-time students as such and how far of higher education students generally? On some issues we are able to report student (and, occasionally, staff) perceptions of the differences between the part-time and the full-time experience. But for the most part we cannot make confident direct contrasts, since we had no control group of full-timers. There is a further complicating factor: nearly all our students were mature. Many of the staff we interviewed found it hard to distinguish the effects of part-time students' maturity from the effects of their part-time status. However, in acknowledging this difficulty, we are reflecting two things: the impossibility of clearly distinguishing full- from part-time and the heterogeneity of part-time experiences, which is such that it does not make sense to lump them all together in a single category and contrast it with full-timers.

The advantages of maturity were strongly signalled by staff interviews. Comments from university D staff were typical: part-time students impressed with their motivation, seriousness and willingness to participate in class; moreover they had the ability to learn from their own and from others' experience. These are unsurprising but very important results.

The category of 'mature' in itself is overstretched, referring sometimes to chronological age limits – 21 for undergraduate entrants, 25 for postgraduate – and sometimes to personal outlook or behaviour. More of our university students were mature in the conventional social sense, say over 30, and this influences both motivation and perceptions of costs and benefits. But maturity is a relative matter. Further education colleges have a student population which is, on average, older than that of universities, but for the staff of the Social Care course at college A, part-time students were not only mature but were to be contrasted with classes of 17-year-olds, where ethos and discipline tended to be closer to a school than they are in a university.

Conversely, the further education students tended more to comment on the staff as being teachers rather than lecturers. In part at least, this reflects the different nature of the two professions, with university staff still more fully concerned with the transmission of knowledge whilst college staff are more concerned with the acquisition of skills. But it is more complex than that. In college A, for example, the teaching involved a strong pastoral component, recognising that many students had been out of education for some time and had not had a strong educational background initially. In the university sector the pastoral side was left more to the administrators of the overall programmes.

Related to this is the fact that university students appeared to be expected to do more outside the classroom than the college students. This may be a function of the size and nature of assignments required (though size is not everything and, for some college students, the completion of assignments was clearly a major affair). The exception to this was Automotive Engineering at college A, but the amount demanded of them was the subject of bitter complaint.

Table 8.1 Course ratings (percentage)

Factor Rating	Excellent	Good	Adequate	Poor	Dk/Na
Course Content	27	52	20	1	0
Unit choice	19	32	27	14	7
Quality of teaching	15	46	31	5	4
Quality of learning materials	18	40	33	7	2
Support services	7	23	28	9	34
Library book availability	5	21	30	19	26
Proximity to home/work	21	32	28	8	12
Vary study hours to suit	30	26	20	12	12
Study at home	39	30	17	5	10
Friendly atmosphere	15	44	30	3	7
Fees	5	34	39	7	14
Sample n (100%)	556	556	556	556	556

General perceptions

We asked students to rate their course on eleven different course factors, from teaching through support services to proximity of the institution and its atmosphere. We offered a four-point rating scale from 'excellent' to 'poor'.

The overall picture is positive for the institutions. On most factors the positive ratings clearly outweighed the negative. On course content, for example, nearly 80 per cent rated their own course 'excellent' or 'good'. This general verdict was confirmed by the interviews, where the clear majority expressed definite satisfaction.

There were three factors which did not have an overall approval rating, each significant in its own way. First, only 5 per cent rated fee levels as 'excellent' and another 34 per cent acknowledged them to be 'good'. The most common view (40%) was that they were 'adequate'. This is probably as much as could be expected. Even where people consider that they are getting excellent value for money, the fees themselves are not likely to attract actual applause. But there are some interesting sectoral differences. Over 10 per cent of college students did not know what their fees were and a further 20 per cent marked this as not applicable, which can only mean that they did not pay their own fees, without this indicating whether or not they knew how high they were. This lack of awareness is confirmed by the interview evidence, where students were commonly uncertain what was being paid. It is only in the university sector that there is any serious indication of unhappiness, with 11 per cent indicating that they found the fee levels 'poor'.

Judgements on fee levels are notoriously subjective, however. The interviews revealed considerable difficulties with fee payments amongst college A Social Care students. The institution and its staff were concerned, for different reasons, about the number of students falling into debt – one result being that the college is now invoicing them earlier. This reminds us that it is not only the level of fees but the flexibility of payment systems which affects students.

More than half (55%) of OU students considered the fee levels 'excellent' or 'good', compared with 35 per cent and 28 per cent for the other universities and the colleges respectively, and almost four in five got no support from employers, whereas 40 per cent of other university students and nearly 60 per cent of college students received at least some support. When this is set against the modal fee levels paid by OU students, of £144 and £288, it amounts to a substantial vote of confidence in the OU. (As a minor counterbalance to this, it is curious to note that 14% of OU students felt that they had experienced 'no significant educational benefits' so far and only 27% said that the educational benefits had been 'very significant'. These contrast with equivalent figures of 8% and 40% for the college sector and 12% and 35% for other universities.)

The second factor which did not meet with widespread approval was the availability of library books. Only 26 per cent thought that this was better than 'adequate', well outweighed by the nearly half who found them only 'adequate' or 'poor'. These absolute judgements on a specific facility can be complemented by broader comparative data from our interviews, which suggested that very few of the part-timers thought that they had better facilities than full-timers. Where they felt able to judge, they generally perceived themselves to have less access to library and other facilities.

Generally, universities were perceived to have better facilities than colleges. This may have had something to do with different traditions of part-time modes – colleges have a long track record of catering for part-timers but this has traditionally been more in the day-release mode, so evening or even twilight part-time study may not be accompanied by library and other facilities being open, as is the case at college A. But the main reason is presumably the higher funding for universities. One member of college B's staff, when asked whether part-time students have the same access to facilities as full-timers, replied that she was tempted to say 'What facilities?' Like most colleges, college B did not have a lot of extra-curricular facilities, though what they did have was technically open to part-timers. This sectoral gap is most noticeable in respect of library facilities, which were generally rated higher by university than college students.

However, the fact that facilities exist does not mean that they are available to part-timers. Availability has two aspects: the objective and the subjective. Formally, the library may be open, but the students may not make much use of it, as in university C where one Health Studies student acknowledged the hours as well as the facilities to be good but preferred to use her local library with its much poorer provision because of the contrasting attitudes amongst the staff in the two places. So, despite the sectoral difference in the formal availability of facilities, the issue is one which cuts across sectors. Some students –

for example, most of those in Business Studies – had access to facilities such as computers, or even secretarial assistance, at their place of work and this affected the importance they attributed to the institution's provision of facilities.

The third negative factor rating has a different significance. Student support services were rated 'good' or 'excellent' by 30 per cent and 'adequate' or 'poor' by 37 per cent. Just as significant as the negative balance, however, is the fact that almost a quarter of students did not feel that they knew enough to be able to answer the question and for a further 9 per cent it was considered 'not applicable'. In other words, for one-third of the students, support services were simply not a relevant factor. Given all the emphasis placed on guidance and other forms of support in recent educational policy literature, this is a significant finding.

It is strengthened by the responses to a more detailed question on sources of support generally. We asked whether students drew on academic counsellors, course lecturers or tutors; on friends, partners or family members; and on work colleagues or employers. We then asked which was the *main* source of support. The results are quite clear: domestic sources were far more significant than academic or work ones. Academic counsellors figured hardly at all, except in the OU where over a third of the students used them. Course tutors were used in over half the cases but the most common source was spouse or partner, drawn on by three in five students. The student's spouse or partner was the main source of support in 45 per cent of the cases, compared with a mere 1 per cent who looked on an academic counsellor as the main source. Other students were the main support source for 14 per cent. If we cluster the remaining categories into academic, family/friends and work, the figures are 19 per cent, 56 per cent and 7 per cent respectively.

There is an interesting gender difference in relation to support. Men relied more on academic sources for support whilst women looked to friends and family. The course tutor was named as the main support by 27 per cent of men, compared with 9 per cent of women, whilst 65 per cent of women looked first to friends or family, compared with 46 per cent of men. The social, and socially structured, character of support services is very evident. In addition, as some of our individual examples show, men may draw on domestic support – for example in having assignments word-processed – but

Table 8.2 Course ratings of 'excellent' or 'good' by sector (percentages)

Factor	Colleges	Universities	OU
Course content	63	78	95
Unit choice	30	48	77
Quality of teaching	51	63	70
Quality of learning material	35	48	93
Support services	12	17	64
Library book availability	25	31	19
Proximity to home/work	61	61	35
Vary study hours to suit	35	44	94
Study at home	48	61	99
Friendly atmosphere	58	61	58
Level of fees	28	35	56

take it for granted and, therefore, not recognise it alongside the support they received in the institution.

With these three exceptions, then, the general picture was one of student satisfaction. However, there were significant variations across sectors, as seen in Table 8.2. Universities tended to receive higher ratings than colleges and the specialist part-time provider, the OU, appeared to justify its specialist position by scoring higher than the other sectors on almost every index of student satisfaction.

A huge majority (95%) of OU students rated their course content 'excellent' or 'good', compared with 78 per cent of other university students and 61 per cent of college students. Equivalent figures for quality of teaching were 70 per cent, 63 per cent and 51 per cent respectively and for quality of learning materials the gap was enormous at 93 per cent, compared with 48 per cent and 35 per cent. This latter is not surprising given the scale on which the OU operates in its production of materials and the resources it is able to put into them. Also not surprising is the higher rating given to the choice of unit it offers. When it comes to student support services, the OU's experience and structure also makes its high rating of 64 per cent judging them 'excellent' or 'good' predictable but the gap between this and 17 per cent for universities and 12 per cent for colleges is very striking. In both the latter two sectors, over 40 per cent said that they did not know about support services or found the question was not applicable.

There were few sectoral differences in response to a question on the atmosphere of the institution. In all three sectors, close to three out of five students found the atmosphere friendly and welcoming. However, and perhaps curiously, here again the OU could be considered to score higher than the others since over 20 per cent found its atmosphere 'excellent', compared with 13 per cent for each of the other two, and only 22 per cent 'adequate' or 'poor', compared with 36 per cent and 41 per cent for other universities and colleges. The disparity in the aggregate figures is explained by the 18 per cent of OU students for whom this question was not applicable. This does raise the issue of what is considered to be the 'atmosphere' of an institution which teaches primarily in distance mode, but it is not a meaningless question – OU students may have been referring to their study centres or to the tone of correspondence, the telephone contacts or the materials themselves which they received from the institution.

Students in some courses felt themselves to be distinctly more marginal than in others, even within the same institution. This is best illustrated by the contrast between Combined Studies and Health Studies at university C. Combined Studies students were enrolled on their modules on an infill basis. This was negotiated on their behalf by the programme administrators, who conducted a series of bilateral negotiations with the respective course tutors. Decisions on whether a place was available could be delayed until very close to the beginning of term. This meant that not only was the student not sure what they would be able to study in the coming semester but, almost more importantly, they might not know when they would be expected to be on campus, and this could create major difficulties where they have work or domestic commitments.

Once they are into the course their experience may be marginalising, for two main reasons: one curricular/pedagogic and one social but with significant implications for their educational experience. First, the tutor may teach to the programme rather than the module – he or she may assume that the students have attended previous modules and are studying in a conventional sequential mode, rather than the more aggregative mode which characterises Combined Studies. Second, even though the full-time curriculum is also modular with options and variations, more of the full-time students will know each other and have studied together before starting a given module. The part-timers can, therefore, find themselves isolated at the outset and this may be accentuated by the fact that they often cannot participate fully in the social activities of the class, even at the level of having coffee together whilst waiting for the next class to begin. This is not a matter of social convenience alone since useful learning and information exchange may occur in these interstices. Being out of the regular class body meant that students could also miss out on information from the course tutor. One student, the only part-timer on a computer studies module, did not hear about the rescheduling of a test and, as a result, had to take it in an office where staff were having their coffee break. She failed. (Against this should be set the testimony of one staff member with involvement in both the Combined Studies and Health Studies courses who spoke of having 'had to adjust students' assessment timetables often over the years because children have become ill or the husband's lost his job'.)

In Health Studies, on the other hand, although the programme was modular, it was dominated by part-timers and there was no sense of marginality, as least as far as the course was concerned (though there may have been in respect of the institution – several Health Studies students portrayed themselves as semi-detached, for example in relation to the library and other facilities). Indeed, several students referred to having had information about the module they were about to take passed on to them by students who had already done it, showing that there was clearly some kind of functioning network.

The perception of marginality was sometimes shared by staff, but speaking from a different angle. At university D, in one of the departments, staff offered a picture of the full-time student as the 'ideal' model because of the operation of a 'departmental culture' which gave the student a particular identity and affiliation with the opportunity to read round the subject. Very few part-time students said that they considered themselves as 'students' and all had other major commitments to which they generally accorded higher priority than their studies, so this concept of education as an immersion in a culture was not available to them. There is, however, another side to this, namely that the part-timers were correspondingly protected from the negative aspects of the full-time student culture:

> Alan is a 39-year-old divorced man living with his parents. He pushes typologies of part-time activity to their limit since he has five different part-time jobs – a different one each evening from Monday to Thursday plus one on Saturday morning – as well as doing Combined Studies one day a week. This course, moreover, will enable him to complete a degree since he started out doing a medical degree several years ago. So it is not surprising that he calls himself a 'full-time part-timer' but, in fact, he is referring only to his studying, so the jobs he does have to be 'really part-time'. In spite of this sense of commitment, he feels 'a bit out of it', without as much access as full-timers to materials or to opportunities to thrash things out with other students, though they are friendly towards him. Library resources are generally excellent but the number of books in the part-time collection is inadequate and in his single full day at the university he doesn't have time to make proper use of the facilities.

Perceptions of course quality can vary within institutions. Thus Accounting in college B received generally favourable verdicts from the students whilst Graphic Design in the same place had a far more mixed response. Such intra-institutional variation is natural and not specific at all to part-time study. We should also note that the Graphic Design course was in a transitional period with a high level of staff change, which naturally influenced the provision. More significant is the variation between Combined Studies and Health Studies at university C, bearing in mind the result reported above on marginality. In spite of their marginality, Combined Studies students reported greater satisfaction than did those in Health Studies, where some of the teaching received strongly adverse comments. However, 'course' level is too crude to do this justice since the comments were directed only at one or two specific modules rather than at the course as a whole. Indeed, it was noticeable that the respondents on Health Studies were not really able to comment on the course as such but only on individual modules and their responses were to individual teachers rather than the programme as a whole.

Intra-institutional differences in marginality were also evident in college A, where Social Care students saw themselves as completely cut off from the college, arriving at twilight, never mixing with other students and having access only to basic facilities in that the availability of a microwave oven to make drinks was an issue since the cafeteria was shut by the time they arrived.

Finally, variations between individual responses on course quality were striking. Within university C, one student referred to the library facilities as 'a joke' whilst the next called them 'excellent' and within Combined Studies, one referred to them as 'dreadful' whilst the next found them 'very good'. As anyone who has been involved with student feedback will recognise, it is indispensable but can be contradictory.

External influences on quality perceptions

Student satisfaction is not a function of the teaching alone or, indeed, of the set of factors listed above. The survey data do not capture the contexts within which specific courses operate, such as the nature of the local or the occupational labour market. Some of the student dissatisfaction in Health Studies at university C derived from the feeling that they were being almost forced to enrol for a qualification which, in their view, would not add a great deal to their professional competence or do wonders for their professional prospects. Moreover, as one of the staff counsellors pointed out, some of the anxieties and negative feelings were associated with the stresses of change within the NHS which were transposed onto the course. Thus the dice were somewhat loaded against the course tutors from the start. Nevertheless, against that background there was still significant variation in the warmth with which different modules were received. Moreover, as with motivation, satisfaction can change over time and more than one Health Studies student reported that their general satisfaction with the course had grown or, to put it a different way, that their initial disenchantment had been at least partially replaced by a sense of satisfaction at studying successfully.

Some of the variation in perceptions may be an indirect function of the course content, in the following sense. Where there is a clear professional link, the teacher's expertise is more transparent than where the course is more purely academic. This is accentuated in the case of part-time study since the student returns to work immediately following the class and is therefore in a position to make a rapid judgement on the quality of the teaching, at least as he or she perceives it, and on other items, such as the appropriateness of the technology used. The more academic the course is, the harder it is for the student to mobilise his or her professional experience to query, explicitly or secretly, the authority of the teacher. This does not insulate the teacher against criticism but gives the source of student dis/satisfaction a different character.

There are wider influences on the quality of student experiences. Most of the students doing the Automotive Engineering HNC at college A were on social security. Their experience was highly coloured by the problems they experienced with DSS offices over payments and their availability for work. The recurrent interviews were seen as a major hassle, especially at times when assignments were due, and, as a result, the hours they were doing college work clearly encroached on their availability for the kind of work the DSS is interested in. Although there is a certain amount which the college can do to improve their access to benefits, including providing good information on their entitlements, much of this is outwith the institution's sphere of influence.

Standards

Both in universities and colleges there is the question of whether part-time students are being assessed at the same level as full-timers. However, there is a strong sectoral dimension to it. As far as internal procedures are concerned, in both colleges students remarked that assessment procedures were often loose, work was not marked and handed back quickly, and in more than one college course students were still waiting months later for the results of earlier assignments, so that they might not even be clear of their eligibility for a final award. Here too there was individual variation: an Engineering student reported that he had pressed for tighter grading of assessments, including firmer adherence to deadlines, and attracted the opprobrium of his fellow students for doing so. Flexibility can be interpreted as slackness and there is a tension between making allowances for the extra pressures under which part-timers find themselves and not allowing different standards to apply for the same qualification.

In the universities the issue of comparability covered admission requirements as well as assessment standards and course content. In university D staff were concerned that greater integration might involve a danger that the different part-time arrangements would undermine established quality whilst students were more worried that uniform procedures across part-time and full-time provision might in practice be biased towards full-timers. One staff member felt that standards for evening students might be affected because only General rather than Honours degrees were available.

The issue of standards arises in another context. One college B employer was unsympathetic to the idea of tying pay awards to the award of qualifications because there was no guarantee of the quality of the certificated competence. This was, very indirectly, supported by a Combined Studies student at university C. She had previously done an HNC which she regarded as a 'doddle' by comparison – they were given so many chances under continuous assessment that it had been difficult to fail. This suggests the rather paradoxical conclusion that degrees which, by their nature, tend to be less closely tied to specific jobs or occupations may nevertheless be given stronger credibility in relation to pay scales. This is only hinted at in our evidence but the size of the graduate/non-graduate differential at national level, does something to support the point. The two points are connected by the issue of continuous assessment. In one college it was reported that 100 per cent assessment influences the student/ tutor relationship since the student's result then depends almost wholly on the tutor's judgement.

In general, it appears that part-time students were likely to aim to pass rather than to excel in their course – satisficing, in other words. Since we have no comparable data for full-timers, we cannot judge whether this attitude is particularly pronounced amongst part-timers. It is, of course, explicable by reference to the other pressures which they are under and the fact that the studying component of their lives is rarely the dominant one, so that achievement here is subordinated to other priorities.

Programme length and recognition of prior learning

The university students were all enrolled on degrees, though not all on Honours degrees, with the slight exception of some of the Health Studies students in university C who may finish up with a professional diploma despite the encouragement of staff for them to complete a degree. The college students, on the other hand, were currently going only for a Certificate, although a proportion of them are likely to carry on to a higher level. (In Accounting at college B, for example, staff expected many students to return to the college to take professional qualifications since the HNC would give them some exemptions from the foundation level of ACCA.) However, and as a consequence, the recognition of prior learning becomes a more significant issue for university students than it is for college ones. Even though part-time courses do not necessarily last twice as long as full-time ones, the stretch of five or six years is too much for many. University D awards an eighth of the General degree credit requirement to those who already have a degree, in whatever discipline, which gives graduates a slight start. In university C, in Health Studies, it was absolutely decisive for many that their previous awards and experience are recognised and a significant task for the course organiser was to ensure that this happens.

The Combined Studies programme offered particular advantages in this respect. One student had already done five years of a medical degree at a different (pre-1992) university but had not completed it and therefore had no qualification. The Combined Studies arrangements meant that with two more years part-time study he could hope to finish with an MA or BSc. This relatively modest amount of extra study would transform him, statistically and personally, from a drop-out to a university graduate.

In Accounting at college B accreditation of prior learning (APL) was formally on offer and one staff member was trained in its application. However, it appeared that, on the one hand, no students had taken advantage of this whilst, on the other hand, several of them felt that they were covering ground already familiar to them. So working out the most effective application of APL remains a difficult issue.

Being a consumer: authority without power

We have already noted how part-time students were seen by their institutions in more of a customer role,because they are more likely to be paying their own way and because they tend to be busier than full-timers with other responsibilities. This can bring with it some measure of influence. However, as in other spheres of the consumer society, it would be wrong to exaggerate their power as consumers – they may be poorly organised and the costs of exercising or attempting to exercise their rights as customers may be considerable or, at least, not worthwhile:

> Connie works as photographic/reprographics technician and studies Graphic Design at College B one day a week. She is employed and has her fees paid by a local university. She was highly critical of the way the course was run in the first year. She felt that part-time students were not given enough time or support from staff and she was left to work on her own a lot with inadequate information about learning outcomes and course content. She felt that both her and her employer's complaints to the sector head were brushed aside. However, the teaching itself was fair, she enjoys the course and she picks up useful ideas from the other students.

Work/study relationships

The relationship between work and studying is often two-way. We looked to discern whether it was predominantly from work to study or vice versa. For some students, studying helped their work as they learnt things which they could apply directly or indirectly at the workplace. For others, the reverse was broadly the case: they bring to their study experience, from work and elsewhere, and were less likely to find study relating directly to their work. In some cases this was predictable because of the course content, for example in the case of English Studies at university D, but even in the more vocational fields study was less likely to be interleaved with daily practice. In fact, the nurse training which many of the Health Studies students had received followed a model of three weeks of teaching followed directly for ten weeks by practice in the wards of what they had learnt. Then the block was changed. It was still 13 weeks in total but split between teaching for ten weeks and preparation for assessment for three, with a far looser connection with work, if any, since it depended on what the individual student's job content was at the time.

This loosening was encapsulated in a comment from one of the Health Studies students on the shift of nurse education into higher education, mostly full-time:

> We're getting students from the [university] out just now on place-ment. These are third year students who, if successful, register as nurses in September and this is their first practical experience of working with people with a learning disability. When I was a third-year student I was running wards and, personally speaking, I feel that's what nursing is about – the practical stuff. Not so much the carrying out of procedures but the actual working with people.

The relationship between work and study was also affected not only by the nature of the student's occupation but also by the size of the workplace. Thus in Accounting, a student working in a small firm would be likely to have to cover a range of accounting tasks whereas one working in a large firm might be working in a more limited area. The conclusion is not only that the relationship is a two-way one but that it can have features which are not immediately predictable. We expand on this below when dealing with costs and benefits.

There is, however, a broader feature of the relationship which deserves comment and which provides one of the strongest contrasts between part-time and full-time students. Although we report the stress which many part-time students experienced in combining their studies with a job and, usually, also with family responsibilities, there is another side to this particular coin: the structural stability which the job provided in their lives. It did this in at least four ways. First, and most materially, it provided them with a relatively stable income, enabling them to sustain a lifestyle which is not too different from those of contemporaries who are not studying. Although full-time students receive a far higher public subsidy because their fees are automatically paid for, their absolute income levels are likely to be lower. Increased levels of student poverty mean that many full-timers are in a very uncertain financial state and this can prejudice their studying significantly. It is both the absolute levels of income and the fact that the money does not come in on a regular monthly or weekly basis which contribute to this. The regularity of the income of most part-timers provided an important stability for them.

Second, the job provided a daily and a weekly structure to their lives which was enabling as well as constraining. The fact that their time was not only limited but outwith their control deprived part-timers of much choice, but provided they can manage to keep on the tracks, the lack of choice may have helped them. The proviso is an important one. It may be harder for part-timers to regain their position once they slip but the full-timers' lack of a job as an external factor structuring their time made it, in one sense, easier for the overall structure of their study time to collapse.

Third, part-timers were more likely to have a sense of where their occupational career might be leading and of the role which education might play in this. As we say elsewhere, the expectations of future benefits were often quite vague but, compared to those outside the labour market altogether, jobholders' awareness of career prospects was relatively high and this helped give them some sense of purpose.

Fourth, the fact that part-time students had multiple commitments – to a job and/or family as well as to the course – could help to reduce the stress associated with any one of them. Several part-time students commented that however difficult they found keeping up with course reading and assignments, the pressure was much easier to bear because the course was not, in the last analysis, the most important thing in their lives. However badly they fared on the course, their job or family life would not normally be directly affected. Conversely, the course provided relief from the pressures of work or family. Many welcomed the structured opportunity to 'switch off' from their other concerns on the evenings when they had classes to attend.

These factors explain, for example, unexpected differential drop-out rates in the Engineering course at college A, where the staff noted that full-timers were placed in a dilemma if they had the prospect of a proper job which might not still be there when they finished the course and where full-timers were in more straitened financial circumstances than part-timers. This phenomenon – the part-timer benefiting from relative financial stability and a stronger time structure – is one which may prove to be increasingly significant when the financial status of full-time students is still changing and when the labour market is as uncertain as it currently is.

Family rhythms

The pattern of any student's life is a function of the interaction between classroom and personal study, employment and domestic responsibilities. In the case of part-timers, the latter two were more likely to play a significant part – employment because they will often have chosen the part-time route in order to retain a job (though we recognise that many full-time students are now working significant hours, even in term time) and family responsibilities because they are older, on average, than full-timers.

It is encouraging to report that 84 per cent of the sample said that their families were supportive, 12 per cent that they were indifferent and less than 1 per cent that they actively opposed their participation. However, this does not mean that fitting studying into domestic timetables did not pose significant problems: 'Finding time has been difficult but it's all about forming habits'. (Combined Studies student, university C)

Students develop their own routines and these have a wide variety of shapes. Tracing these in detail would have been beyond our resources but our data suggest that there are two common patterns. Some students study on a predominantly weekly pattern, so there are set times when they study which remain broadly consistent week by week. Other students' routines are determined primarily by the course rhythm. Typically, this involved a relatively stress-free period in which there is a minor weekly routine of class attendance followed by a major burst of activity in order to fulfil the necessary assessments. In this, part-timers probably do not differ from full-timers.

However, stress and the pressure on routines did not derive only from the course requirements but from home life. In the first place, attendance at college may require childcare arrangements, as Steve's case below (pp.162–4) graphically illustrates. An Accounting student whose husband ran his own company and was not available for childcare had a babysitter in to allow her to attend evening classes. (The student did the books for the family company – an interesting example of a triple intersection between study, work and domestic life.) There are also travel arrangements, where there are competing claims on a single car.

At home, there are a range of competing claims. As one Social Care student said, 'the moment I get the books out, all hell breaks loose'. Others referred to the juggling in which they had to engage in order to fit the studying in with other domestic activities, with greater or lesser degrees of friction. Broadly speaking, such timetables take one of two forms. Concurrent meshing means that our students were studying alongside children or spouses, sharing domestic space and time. Studying was done as part of the domestic routine, perhaps displacing watching TV. Sequential arrangements refer to patterns where space or time opened up only after other members of the family departed, usually to bed, and the room or the computer then became free. One student worked upstairs at the computer until his wife came up to bed, whereupon he would transfer downstairs, sometimes even taking the computer down with him – not exactly a model of sociability but a requirement of the demands on him.

Usually, the tension is with other family activities which have nothing to do with education, but it can occur where other members of the family are also studying. This can have positive effects for all. In one case, a youthful (44-year-old) grandfather bought a computer both to help him work for his HNC and to learn alongside his grandchildren.

> Ann and Philip are married and both are studying social care at college A one or two evenings a week. They have no children. Both work as supervisors in a day care centre and hope for promotion when they have completed the course. The employer pays their fees but their line managers take no interest in their studies – in fact they appear resentful as they are themselves unqualified. She reports that domestic pressures and the uneven distribution of assignments make it difficult for her to study at home, with the weekly requirement varying from 0 to 25 hours. She prefers to study on her own and, therefore, to do this at home when Philip is out since he tries to involve her in the coursework, comparing notes and generally discussing progress. He also feels unsupported at work and regrets what he sees as the excessive latitude allowed to students on the submission of assignments, which makes structuring difficult.

The patterns need to be traced on a template which goes beyond the daily routine. The fullest example of this comes from one of our family interviews, carried out with the wife of Steve N, an Engineering student at college A. It illustrates:

- the complexity of a family schedule where a parent is studying

- the collective effort involved in Steve's actually studying

- the time/money nexus: it is his time as much as the money which impedes them from making more rapid progress with the house

- expectations of concrete advantages are not high – it might reduce chances of him being made redundant and might help him get promotion, but these are quite vague.

Household structure

The family moved house two years ago and one of the consequences of Steve's studying is that they have not been able to do it up as fast as they would have liked – plans for returfing the garden and building a wall are on hold. The front door opens straight into the living area – a sitting-room with dining-area as the bar of the L, leading into the kitchen. The interior layout matters because Steve does his studying at the dining room table, which is at the centre of the ground floor accommodation. The kids usually eat off their knees in front of the TV.

The immediate family is Mr and Mrs N, Laurence (8) and Deirdre (6). But the wider family is crucial. Mrs N's parents live close by (but not next door – a 15-minute drive) and both play vital roles. Her mother retired from her job as a care assistant when the first grandchild arrived and her father works in a printing company.

Timetables

The daily family schedule is as follows:

06.50   Steve leaves for work.

              Mrs N takes kids to school, does her own thing – 'gallivanting' – in the morning, except on Friday when she helps in Deirdre's computer class.

12.00   She gives the kids lunch, takes them back to school and, three days a week, drives on to her job as a midwife at the Hospital, where she works back shift, 13.45–22.00. On Tuesday afternoon she helps in Laurence's knitting class.

15.00   Granddad picks kids up from school, takes them to his house.

17.00   On most days, Steve comes home and grandfather delivers kids on his way. On Mondays and Wednesdays, though, he goes straight to college, so doesn't get home till 19.45 – in which case, if Mrs N is working, granddad delivers the kids on his way to nightshift instead. On other days, if Steve cannot get a lift home from college, Mrs N or her father will pick him up.

22.30   Mrs N gets home.

The weekly pattern involves:

Tuesday evening: Laurence goes to karate, Deirdre goes to Girls' Brigade.

Thursday: At teatime both kids swim then Laurence goes to Boys' Brigade.

Saturday morning: Deirdre goes to dancing, Laurence goes to football.

Saturday afternoon: Mrs N takes the kids to the pictures to give Steve   some peace to study.

Two out of every six weeks Mrs N works night shift, 21.45 to 07.45, three nights one week and two the following. This is at the weekend. Being part-time, she fits her shifts around the full-timers.

At present, Steve does Wednesday evenings and Friday afternoons at college. Hopefully, he'll get the first HNC in June. But at the start of the new academic year he'll be back doing Monday evenings, Wednesday evenings and Friday afternoons for another two years.

Motive

Steve started studying in 1993. 'I think he was just worried about the job situation, with them laying off so many men. There was people with better qualifications, better suited to jobs. Him being that wee bit older and he didn't have the opportunity when he was younger. He just came home one day and said he fancied doing it. I don't think it will prevent him from losing his job – if he's got to go, he'll go – but at the end of the day he'll have his HNC behind him. That and if there's a possibility of him getting promotion'.

How did you feel? 'I was a bit worried about having to request all these Fridays off but the work has been very good, they've been very accommodating and I have managed to get most Fridays off. There have been days when we've been stuck but we've usually had someone to fall back on, whether it's one of my friends or one of my brothers'.

Current impact

'He spends quite a lot of time studying, especially when it comes to exam time. He'll have everything everywhere and we'll have big boxes of books that we never had before that we've had to find places to fit. This cabinet that used to be full of bits and pieces is now crammed full of leaflets and notes and things'.

Is there a financial impact? 'Not really, because he's still working and the employer pays the fees'.

As for her own career: 'I've had to put it on hold, on the back burner. I'm hoping to a do a degree in neonatology'. This has not actually been set up yet, so she could not have started before next year anyway. If she does start then, he will still be studying and that will take some 'jiggery-pokery'!

What are the other family attitudes? 'The kids are not bothered. It's just that he's in there studying and they're out there playing. My parents kid him on – "all this hassle and I don't know if it's worth it" – but when I told my mum that he was not going to go and do this next HNC because it was going to mean another two years and he'd be out on Monday night and Wednesday night she went crazy: "Oh for goodness sake tell him he's to do it, tell him to phone me and I'll tell him he's to do it". So they're very supportive although they kid him on'.

Support comes from the rest of the family (see earlier, on childcare). But in addition, 'I do his drawings sometimes. But that's all, and I do the proofreading. My mum does the typing, she's got a computer. I'll read through what he's written. It means nothing to me, though I know everything about ISO9000 now, quality kitemarks and that sort of thing. I'll do his proofreading, check his spelling'. He writes his essays out in rough, his mother-in-law takes them away, tries to make sense of all the arrows etc. – she's never off the phone.

Importantly, Steve receives support from his line manager, who is also doing a course.

Children are obviously a major claim on students' time. Moreover, it is harder for their claims to be settled into a fixed pattern, so that interruptions are more probable. On top of their individual and unpredictable (in the temporal rather than the psychological sense) demands, study can pose a threat to the collective family rhythm. More than one student referred to Saturday as a day when they were expected to join in family activities rather than tuck themselves away to get on with their studying. But children are not the only type of domestic responsibility. Reflecting broad demographic trends, several students had elderly dependants who made similar claims, implicitly or explicitly.

As with motivation, domestic attitudes can change over time. Broadly speaking, two trajectories emerge. On the one hand, family members are initially accepting but find, over time, that the demands on the students' time and energies impinge undesirably on their own claims. On the other hand, and more commonly, there is some alarm or even resistance at first, but this diminishes as new routines are established:

> Laura is a Business Studies student from university D. Initially her husband was strongly against it and complained that he and their daughter were being deprived of quality time. The first three semesters were 'hell'. Since then he has softened. She says her daughter couldn't care less – but, perhaps, takes a bit of pride in mum. Laura has a cleaning lady couldn't manage the course otherwise. She has a desk in the same room as her husband (who works a lot from home) but can only work when he is not there. She has a routine. Friday is 'family day' but she spends Sundays 'with my head in a book', even when preparing meals, etc. They eat a lot more convenience foods now. Social life is affected. They never invite anyone for dinner during a semester.

Even where no children or other family are involved, domestic rhythms can be a problem. This is true even where the partner is also a student and even where this is on the same course, as was the case with two of our college A students. There were positive aspects to this, obviously, as the couple could discuss common issues but their patterns of studying at home did not mesh completely since the woman preferred to have long blocks of solitude whilst the man wanted to check across more frequently.

Advantages and disadvantages

One of the objectives of our study was to investigate the costs and benefits of studying part-time, for students, institutions and employers. Here we concentrate on the students; the institutional perspective has been largely covered in Chapter 5 and the employer perspective will be dealt with in the following chapter.

There are two interrelated issues we should address before reporting on this. In both the survey and the interviews we asked students for their current perceptions about the costs and benefits of part-time study and their anticipations of future costs and benefits. The survey dealt only passingly with explicit contrasts between full- and part-time, so their responses show the costs and benefits of studying part-time rather than not studying at all. But when it came to the interviews it was not always easy to be clear whether the emphasis of the responses was on study as such or on its part-time nature. Second, we found that responses to the cost/benefit question tended to be narrow and to repeat points previously made. We therefore switched to asking about advantages and disadvantages rather than costs and benefits.

Students who took part in the survey saw definite benefits of various kinds. They also reported costs, in many cases significant costs, but the overall verdict was unambiguously favourable, with benefits outweighing costs. We asked about several different types of costs and benefits – financial, career, personal, domestic, social and educational. The relationships between these are not always obvious. For example, the results on career benefits do not correlate exactly with financial benefit and this fits very well with our qualitative evidence, which shows that students may expect no financial return but still think that they are occupationally better off.

As far as costs were concerned, the highest price appeared to be a personal one. Nearly 70 per cent said that the personal costs were either 'significant' or 'very significant'. This was followed by financial costs, at 56 per cent, although over half of these said that the costs were 'very significant' whereas only one in three of those who flagged up personal costs rated them this highly.

Once again, interpretations of what amounts to a 'significant' cost are bound to be subjective. In some instances the financial costs involved entail the student getting a second job in order to make ends meet. In others it will only be 'significant' in the sense that someone paying for a more expensive night out than they are used to would find it so. How is one to rate the fact that a family could not go on holiday in the summer because of study commitments, as one of our English Studies students at university D noted?

Costs vary according to age. Almost uniformly, the various costs were considered to be more significant by those in the middle age range, 31–40. For example, 26 per cent of these reported 'very

Table 8.3 Costs of studying (percentages)

Type of cost	Very significant	Significant	Not significant
Financial	21	35	44
Personal	20	49	31
Home life	14	42	44
Social life	16	37	48
Work life	9	26	66

significant' personal costs, compared with 17 per cent of the younger and 15 per cent of the older age groups. This, of course, does not reflect chronological age as such but the classic lifecycle squeeze as people with families and other commitments find these competing with their study. Only one in three of the middle age group said that there were 'no significant costs' to their home life.

Not surprisingly, whether or not the employer contributes to the fees made a difference. Only 10 per cent of those who received such contributions reported the financial cost to themselves as 'very significant', and 64 per cent said there was 'no significant cost' whereas, of those who received no such support, 29 per cent reported 'very significant' financial costs and almost the same proportion (30%) 'no significant financial costs'. This explains why fewer college than university students reported 'significant' financial costs since more of the former receive employer support.

There was a fairly clear, though not large, class split when it comes to financial costs. One in two of those in managerial and professional occupations said that studying incurred 'no significant financial costs' for them whereas the figure for technical and clerical employees dropped to around 36 per cent.

Women respondents consistently reported higher costs than men, though not always by very much. Thus 67 per cent of women said that they are incurring 'significant' or 'very significant' financial costs, compared with 46 per cent of men. On personal costs, the figures were 79 per cent and 58 per cent. For home life, the gap was smaller at 61 per cent and 50 per cent for women and men respectively:

> Stephanie is married with one child. She attends college B one day and one evening a week, on the Accounting HNC. She is a self-employed book-keeper, currently doing her husband's books. He is supportive of her studying, predictably enough, and she gets peace and space at home. The flexibility of self-employment allows her to plan her coursework. But she has to pay for a baby-sitter for her evening study and at present she doesn't have enough money to pay for next year's fees, though she definitely hopes to progress to the HND and beyond in order to become a qualified accountant.

The interviews confirmed these variations in other ways. For example, stress levels varied between courses within the same institution. Almost all the Business Studies students reported quite high stress levels and difficulties in reconciling studies with some aspect of the rest of their lives, whilst none of the English Studies students did. A similar intra-institutional divergence was apparent in college B where Accounting students reported very little stress compared with Graphic Design, though both are doing vocationally-oriented HNCs.

As far as current benefits are concerned, one-third of the survey respondents reported 'very significant' educational benefits and nearly the same proportion 'very significant' personal benefits. Only 12 per cent reported 'no significant educational benefits' and 18 per cent 'no significant personal benefits'. It is very clear, on the other hand, that there is no immediate financial payoff to studying – 86 per cent said that there had been 'no significant financial benefit' and only just over one in ten reported 'very significant' benefits to their working lives. However, a further 36 per cent reported some 'significant' benefit to their working life, so when allowance is made for the numbers who had no occupation-related motives, the picture looks more positive and, as we shall see, it changes considerably when we come to anticipated benefits.

First, the distinctions between vocational and non-vocational benefits are very hard to maintain in any simple fashion. The development of generic skills, for instance at the level of general confidence, spreads across boundaries in ways which the individuals can report on with emphasis but which are almost impossible to measure. Second, several students said that they did not expect direct and positive benefits at work, in the sense that they would gain promotion or extra pay, but that they would improve their chances of retaining jobs in industries or companies where the threat of redundancy was real. This was especially evident in Shipbuilding Engineering, where fluctuations in demand for the product and the competitive nature of the industry meant that there were regular bouts of downsizing. Studying for an HNC would not guarantee continuity of employment but it would raise the probability of being kept on. One student described how colleagues at work had dropped out of courses because they chose, or were obliged, to maintain overtime commitments, which gave them immediate material benefits but at the possible expense of their future job security.

Third, studying can give access to certain types of vocabulary and concepts which do not affect the job in specific ways but which give students a sense of enhanced professionalism, and this in turn affects their motivation and competence. Of course, this kind of outcome could take the form of inflated professional jargon but there is clear evidence that for certain categories, notably in the Social Care course, the positive impact on subjectively undervalued workers was

Table 8.4 Current benefits of studying (percentages)

Type of benefit	Very significant	Significant	Not significant
Financial	5	9	86
Educational	34	55	12
Personal	29	53	18
Home life	3	16	78
Social life	3	19	78
Work life	11	36	53

significant. They felt better because they had a grip on the wider context.

Fourth, as we said earlier, not only is the relationship between work and study two-way but the relationship has an interesting dynamic. Thus progress in a course which is not job-related may encourage the acquisition of new work skills and vice-versa, and these interactions may occur in different directions at different points in the course. We are not able to trace these in any detail but this dynamic needs to be linked to the changes in motivation over time which we have already reported. Moreover, for some students, studying comes as a welcome change from working or from domestic responsibilities, so the difficulties with time management which were regularly referred to were accompanied by (though hardly outweighed by) a positive sense of the value of juggling multiple activities.

Benefits to social life did not come through strongly in the survey responses but the interviews shed more light on how the social impact of studying varied. In Business Studies most students reported that participation in the course had enhanced their social life – they had made some new friends and/or the course had enabled them to enter into new conversational arenas from which they had previously felt excluded. No such effect was reported for English Studies. It should be recalled that these are both evening courses operating under the same conditions of segregation and the same time constraints. Such variation is, perhaps, more surprising when one looks at the course labels as it would have been reasonable to suppose that studying English Studies would open up more conversational and social opportunities, especially since the reasons for doing it were exclusively non-vocational.

There are variations within this general picture. As we have seen in Table 7.4, fewer OU students have vocational motives for studying. Nearly one-quarter of college students have experienced no personal benefits so far, compared with only 13 per cent of OU students – evidence of greater instrumentalism in the former case. If we remove OU students from the picture, the proportions who have already experienced some benefit to their working lives goes up considerably to 51 per cent for university students and 72 per cent for college students.

When we turn to future benefits, over two-thirds (68%) anticipated some financial benefits as a result of studying. An even higher proportion – 88 per cent – anticipated career benefits, this, of course,

Table 8.5 Anticipated benefits (percentages)

Type of benefit	Total	Men	Women
Financial	68	68	68
Educational	87	86	88
Career	88	86	89
Personal	82	76	89
Home life	46	43	47
Social life	42	39	45

could be interpreted negatively or defensively in the sense that studying might help them to avoid redundancy rather than to gain actual reward, but it is a strikingly high figure nonetheless. It outstripped even anticipated personal benefits (82%).

The relationship between motivation and anticipated financial and career benefits merits further comment. Forty per cent of those whose motives were solely personal nevertheless anticipated some financial benefit and this figure climbs to 59 per cent in respect of career benefit. Rightly or wrongly, many people anticipated some kind of career benefit, even though that had not been the purpose of their decision to study. This illuminates the complexity of the relationship and the difficulty in sorting out the world of work from the personal world. One Business Studies student observed during the group discussion:

> Studying it is doing me more good than actually getting it because I don't think it's going to help me in my career. But I think that the fact that on your c.v. you're saying you're studying shows that you're doing something. Whereas as soon as I get a BA it's going to be out of date within a year and it doesn't prove anything when I hit my 50. It

would still look better at that stage [if] you want to go on studying and it suits me now to do it at a slow pace, which is a seven-year period.

There were few significant gender differences in anticipated benefits, perhaps surprisingly few. Women were slightly more optimistic than men on the whole, just as they experienced the costs as being slightly higher. The only gap of significance was in relation to personal benefits, where 13 per cent more women than men anticipated a positive outcome.

How firmly can anyone make the complex set of calculations required to reach an overall judgement about the value of studying? So many of the factors are subjective ones and others are highly unpredictable. Let us take the example of a student who works in the health sector:

> Gillian is doing a Combined Studies degree, which she started in September 1993. She has nearly finished her Level Three modules and is about to take unpaid leave in order to do her Honours level modules. She will do this partly because she wants to do as well as possible but also because psychology is only on offer during the day. It will mean borrowing off her mother as well as taking out a student loan. To date, studying has actually impeded her career – as a nurse she would have wanted to move out into community nursing some time ago but could not have combined this with part-time study. She manages to combine shiftwork with studying, partly because she asks for shifts which are not popular with others, but at the cost of being occasionally irritable at work, and, conversely, her preoccupation with her assignments irritates colleagues, who want to ban her from using the 'A-word'. Gillian gets no assistance with fees, except for help with cash flow – her employer pays them up front and then deducts the money from her pay. She is single so there are no family costs but, on top of the financial, career and personal costs, she feels that she has become more boring – 'social life? I think I remember that'. There is no guarantee that her degree will bring her a better paid, or even more interesting, job and there is a contrast between her level-headed willingness to trade short-term costs against expected longer-term benefits and the actual information on which her calculation of those benefits is based.

It is worth concluding this section by noting the overwhelming optimism on the part of our respondents that the benefits would outweigh the costs – 48 per cent were 'very confident' and 44 per cent 'confident' that they would, leaving only 8 per cent 'doubtful'. When this is set against the costs which we have described, it is a remarkable endorsement.

Emerging issues

Responsibility for the quality of the students' experience

Student satisfaction levels were quite high overall. But their experiences as part-timers were naturally influenced by a very complex, and often unpredictable, set of factors, only some of which fell within the purview of the education system or institution. Families and employers can play a large part and both often bore part of the costs – the former in terms of the personal pressures on the student, the latter more usually in financial terms but also in time. So a first issue concerns how far and in what ways the system, or the institution, can link up with families and/or employers in order to sustain the quality of the experience. Employer support takes myriad forms. This is inevitable and reasonable, given the variety of workplace circumstances. But the variability is not always logical and students can feel unreasonably under-supported in ways which undermine motivation. Public discussion on models of good practice, for example on flexibility of working time patterns, would be a help. Links to families is a more problematical area but some of the link-building which occurs with employers might be extended to include family members.

Status of part-timers

Up to a point, most part-timers seemed quite happy with a relatively marginal status. However, there was a set of quite practical issues to do with access to facilities where positive action could do much to confirm their status as full members of the institution and to provide for the needs of people whose timetables are often very awkward. Staff development may be a significant issue here – ensuring that all staff members who come into contact with part-timers respond to their needs and status. But this is not likely to be solved by individual staff development initiatives. It is more a matter of corporate change. Greater institutional commitment to ensuring that facilities are as available to part-timers as they are to full-timers is a predictable but important issue.

Advantages/benefits: perceptions and reality

Students were generally optimistic about the outcomes of their study, if only in the sense that it will help them preserve their jobs. There was no strong sense from them of impatient demand from employers, actual or prospective, for their greater skills or qualifications. Even where this occured, as in the health sector, it was seen to amount to a requirement for higher qualifications rather than more skills. So there is a twin danger of indifferent demand on the one hand and of credentialism on the other.

Assessment: flexibility and standards

There are some difficulties in applying the same rules in relation to part-timers, in respect of deadlines, and, possibly, in the more significant arena of standards. Because they have legitimate other demands on them (more so than most full-timers), it may be necessary for the tutors, and perhaps the institution, to make allowances. Moreover, where part-time programmes are discrete, it is possible for a discrete set of standards to emerge, even though the syllabus and the teaching staff may be the same as for full-timers. Different does not necessarily mean worse. On the other hand, it would be doing part-timers no favours to allow a two-tier set of standards to develop.

Chapter 9

The Employer Relationship

Starting in

In this chapter we examine the role of employers and their relationships with students and with institutions. We start by describing how the decision to participate in higher education was a function of the employer/student relationship. The way the decision to embark upon studying was taken could colour both parties' attitudes towards learning and responses to the extra work it entails. In most cases there was some degree of negotiation between the parties, explicitly or implicitly. However, our data showed decision making to be more complicated than that.

We interviewed ten employers. Eight were external employers of students whom we had interviewed. A further six of the students whom we interviewed were employed by the institutions at which they studied and we interviewed representatives of the two institutions concerned in their role as employers (universities C and D). From these 14 'sets' of employers and students, only six matched pairs identified the same initiator of the decision to study. No interview students attributed the decision solely to their employer. In the survey students overwhelmingly regarded themselves as in control – 79 per cent of the sample said it was their own decision, 14 per cent said it was a joint decision and only 6 per cent attributed the decision to their employer. However, it is likely that a number of employers would disagree. One institutional employer made the point that while either the employer or the student could initiate the process, the ultimate decision whether or not to support the employee resided with the employer in that institutional approval was needed from not only the employee's head of department but also from the staff development office. Support was normally governed by the trade-off between needs and wants, with needs defined as the university's training policies and wants defined as employees' personal preferences. The latter were, of course, shaped by the former where the employee wished to secure internal advancement. In short, the perceptions of what constituted a joint decision varied between employers and employees; where the employer was involved, it was often in setting guidelines and a framework within which individuals could make their application.

Against this background, the cases where both the student and the employer shared in the decision to study fell into three broad categories. In a few cases employers suggested that the employee embark on a part-time course, possibly in connection with a regular appraisal or performance review, or in a less formal context. The students concerned tended to be young and at the start of their careers and the courses were those (such as the HNCs in Accounting and Electrical Engineering) with a more direct link to career and professional development. This mode is close to the traditional notion of part-time education (typically day-release) for an apprentice or trainee – in the words of a student at college A 'it came with the territory'. However, it was rarely compulsory.

In a larger number of cases employers had an established policy for supporting part-time study but it was largely up to the individual student to take the initiative. Two of the case study courses had been set up in response to employer demand. The Shipbuilding Engineering course at college A was run for employees of a local shipyard and timetabled to fit with their working hours. The employer publicised the course within the workplace, and paid the fees of those who enrolled, but the decision to enter was largely left to the student's initiative. The Health Studies course at university C had been set up in response to employer demand but, following health service changes, employer sponsorship had declined. Students had to take the initiative to enrol and some only found out by accident that their employers had a policy to give partial support for course fees. The university employees who took courses at their own institutions also fall into this category since they took advantage of institutional policies to support staff on part-time courses.

In the largest number of cases the decision was entirely that of the students, who may then have negotiated with their employers for support. The outcome of this negotiation depended on the perceived relevance of the course as well as on more idiosyncratic factors. For example, one student felt she had been refused because her supervisor did not have a higher education qualification himself and felt threatened. Another's employer agreed to give support on the condition that he took Business Studies rather than Computing to introduce managerial skills into a workforce which was already well-represented by IT qualifications. Several students did not ask for support, either because they did not expect a positive response or because they were doing the course for their own benefit and did not want to incur new obligations in respect of it.

Our qualitative data showed how the broad categories of vocational and personal motives to study could be broken down, each into two subsets: 'vocational' into progressive and defensive, and 'personal' into developmental and recreational. *Progressive* motives pertained to various types of job advancement, including seeking pay rises or promotion, a better job, or a career change. *Defensive* motivations occurred when employees felt they needed to compete with colleagues for promotion or retention within the organisation, as was the case with the college A students who worked for a large engineering company, the nature of whose industry was towards periodic bouts of downsizing and re-engagement of staff when more orders came in. *Developmental* motives could also belong to the wider group of combined reasons, though in this context they related to students hoping to increase their self-fulfilment and self- confidence and to other forms of personal development. These motives were often cited by students who had found themselves in some form of rut and who, by studying, were hoping to prove to themselves as much as to others that they could succeed. Finally, *recreational* motives were mentioned by a small minority of students who tended to be reasonably well advanced in their careers, lacking financial worries and using the study experience either as a deliberate form of work-shedding or as a preparation for retirement. However, our main argument is to stress the way in which such categories overlap and interact and how these complexities affect the employer-student relationship, the more so since an individual student may transfer from one category to another in the course of their study.

Employer support

Part-time students suffer from one major form of official dis-crimination in having to find their own fees for higher education. In addition, part-timers are far more likely to be self-funding than full-timers and most of those who are self-funded are also studying in their own time (Tremlett, Thomas and Taylor 1995). So it is important to trace out the different permutations of support – the sources of support and what kinds of support are offered. We do so here in relation to employers as a source.

Employer support falls into three main categories: financial support (course fees, travel, books, equipment, etc), time off work for various reasons and a more pastoral type of support such as offering help and encouragement, showing flexibility over working hours and allowing employees to use work equipment and materials for studying. The model supportive employer would contribute all of these. Not surprisingly, she was not to be found.

Financial support

Overall, employers paid fees for 47 per cent of the sample, books for 14 per cent, travel costs for 11 per cent and equipment for 6 per cent. There was a gender variation: 56 per cent of male students reported having their fees paid, compared with only 38 per cent of females. Those who had fees paid also tended to be younger: 69 per cent of students who were aged 30 or less had fees paid, compared with 33 per cent of 31–40-year-olds and 30 per cent of students over 40. (Interviews confirmed that older students were studying more for personal than for vocational reasons.)

Of students with full-time jobs, 55 per cent had their fees paid by their employers, compared with only 23 per cent of students who worked part-time. Unsurprisingly, there was a clear correlation between fees being paid and whose decision it had been to start studying – 96 per cent of those whose employer decided and 89 per cent of those who reported a joint decision but only 36 per cent of those who said it had been their own decision to study received support for fees. Similarly, 68 per cent of those with vocational reasons, 48 per cent of those with both vocational and personal reasons and only 18 per cent of those with exclusively personal reasons had their fees paid by their employer.

There was, in short, a fairly high level of financial support from employers for part-time study. Fee levels ranged from a few pounds to several hundred annually. At the lower end, clearly, the financial commitment from the employer was fairly trivial. More significantly, this type of support appeared to be increasing but, paradoxically, it was often increasing for reasons of economy. Many employers were reviewing their training expenditure, making it more tightly focused. They were more likely now to build income-foregone (or rather output-foregone) into their calculations and many had concluded that it was cheaper to pay the fees for someone who would study in

**Table 9.1 Rating of course factors as 'excellent' or 'good'
by employer support (percentages)**

Factor	'Excellent' or 'good' rating from:	
	Those with fees paid	*Those with no support*
Course subject/content	65	79
Choice of options/units to suit needs	30	51
Quality of teaching	61	64
Quality of learning materials	38	47
Student support services	10	20
Labs and workshops	27	29
Library book availability	28	28
Proximity to home/work	58	63
Varying hours of study to suit needs	25	54
Opportunity to study at home	44	66
Friendly/welcoming atmosphere	52	67
Level of fees	30	35
Sample n=386 (±2 depending on row)		

their own time than to support a traditional pattern of day release or an equivalent involving time off work. In short, when employers paid for people's time, they wished that time to be spent working for them, but they would pay for employees to spend their own time studying.

Employer support for fees was negatively related to the quality of provision as rated by students. We asked students to rate twelve factors relating to the course they were taking as 'excellent', 'good', 'adequate' or 'poor'. We analysed the responses in more detail in the previous chapter. Here we contrast the proportions giving positive responses ('excellent' or 'good') among those who had fee support from their employers who those who did not. The contrast is shown in Table 9.1.

We see that those students who did not get any financial support from their employers consistently rated course factors higher (in three cases by over 20% higher) than those who had their fees paid. There are a number of possible reasons for this. First, the column 'those with no support' includes 39 students who do not work and a further 18 with part-time jobs. This may help to account for two of the factors with the highest differentials, 'varying hours of study to suit needs' and 'opportunity to study at home', and, perhaps, also for 'choice of options/units to suit needs' if we may assume that it is easier for non-working students to rearrange their other commitments to match the availability of provision.

A few of the self-funding students we interviewed commented that they were more committed to study because they were paying for it themselves. One contrasted his focused attitude now with his experience as a post-school full-time undergraduate, which had been characterised by socialising and cramming for exams. Now he is happily married and has no great desire to socialise with classmates. Several tutors expressed the view that many part-time students, especially those working in service industries, exhibited a 'customer culture' and had greater expectations of the quality of presentation and learning materials than had full-time students.

Time off work

Overall, one-third of students reported that they got time off work for class attendance. Of those who had jobs, 39 per cent were allowed time off work for class attendance, 37 per cent for sitting exams, 20 per cent for exam preparation, 9 per cent for individual study and only 2 per cent for attending summer schools. At the institutional level the variations are striking. Most of the part-time students in college A study by day-release, both daytime and evening modes are in operation in college B and university C for part-time students and most of the part-timers in university D are engaged upon a degree programme taught in the evenings. Among part-time students, 63 per cent of males, but only 37 per cent of females, were allowed time off to attend classes and these students were mostly younger – 69 per cent of those aged up to 30, 19 per cent of those aged between 31 and 40 and 12 per cent of the over-40s were given time off for classes. The gender and age band variations are similar, though slightly less pronounced, for students allowed time off to sit exams and for exam preparation.

The survey data on time off for class attendance do not make allowance for students with different levels of status in their workplace, however, and there is clearly a distinction to be made between formal arrangements for time off on the one hand and informality and flexibility on the other. One English Studies student in university D ran his own company and described himself as semi-retired. Although the course was taught in the evenings, he tried to be assiduous about preparing assignments and commonly spent an additional day per week in the university library, which his seniority and reduced involvement in the day-to-day running of the company made possible. A few of the younger students said that they occasionally used some of their holiday entitlement to complete assignments or prepare for exams and one or two confessed that they surreptitiously did in company time in order to meet deadlines.

How far was the granting of time off linked to a presence or absence of financial support? Only a third of all working students had their fees paid by employers and were allowed time off for class attendance as well. One in four had their fees paid and were given time off for sitting exams and only one in seven had their fees paid and got time off for exam preparation. Interviews with employers suggested that in future, employers would be less likely to offer unconditional support and that students might be required to finance themselves at the start of courses or study in their own time in return for fees being paid to demonstrate commitment. In other words, we are likely to see a growing range of support permutations, with employers and employees contributing different proportions of money and time, according to a range of different contractual or informal arrange- .

Pastoral support

Students were asked to indicate how many from a list of possible sources gave them pastoral support and, from that list, whose support was most important to them. Spouses and partners scored highest, cited by 57 per cent of all students, followed by other students (50%), course tutors (46%), work colleagues (34%) and friends (25%). Employers came sixth, mentioned as a source of pastoral support by 19 per cent of the students – proportionately slightly more by college than university students. Employers were regarded as the most important source of pastoral support by only 3 per cent of the sample (ranked seventh) – favoured again by proportionately slightly more college students, males and students in the lowest age band. Unsurprisingly, amongst those students who were getting their fees paid, employers were rated slightly more highly as a source of pastoral support (fifth, with 35%) and as the most important source of pastoral support (sixth, with 6%).

These findings suggest there is an arms-length relationship between many student employees and their employers (more specifically, the individual who authorised their studying) – a relationship which, in one sense, is likely to be more remote the larger the organisation, though this will be heavily dependent upon its staff development and human resource management policies as larger organisations may be more able to devote resources to these areas. This scenario is even more likely where the objectives of part-time higher education for students and employers do not coincide. The student may aspire to gain a qualification and move on to a better-paid job elsewhere while the employer hopes to have better-trained staff, so, in such circumstances, there is little incentive for the student to seek support from the employer other than to study, fee payment or time off.

Interview data on the extent to which other management support was given were revealing. At least one student from each course (13 in total) reported that their employer or line-manager was supportive or interested in their courses but seven students (covering five of the eight courses) said their employer or line manager was not supportive or interested. Three of the thirteen who received what we call pastoral support were studying HNC Engineering at college A, the course with probably the closest employer links we encountered. Conversely, three of the seven who said they did not get any pastoral support were doing HNCs in Social Care at the same college, the only college course we studied with virtually no discernible employer links.

Employers' demand for part-time higher education

Reasons for supporting part-time higher education

Employers gave two main reasons for supporting part-time higher education among their employees: to enhance the skills and effectiveness of their workforce and to encourage and reward loyalty. These were almost universal responses. A few employers, notably of Social Care students, also saw personal as well as professional development as a goal.

Employers reported a closer attention to the way in which student participation in part-time higher education, as on other courses, fitted with business plans or expectations. Much of the impetus came from a greatly increased concern with quality and advantages were to be measured against this. Just as for the student there could be positive and defensive reasons for engaging in part-time higher education, so there could be for employers. Thus just as they may anticipate direct benefits from a more highly qualified staff, they may also be active in order to prevent themselves from slipping behind the competition reputationally.

For some larger employers, support of part-time higher education students reflected a more or less explicit human resources policy. Some saw it as a means for securing employee loyalty and commitment in a context of job insecurity. In one case training was a reward to staff members who could not be given long-term contracts. One employer tried to maintain a balance between more senior recruits to its accountancy department (who would enter with full-time qualifications) and more junior recruits who would be supported to study part-time. Another said that his company needed 'technicians with intelligence' at HNC level – computers had reduced the need for designers and specialists with high-level knowledge. However, for most of the small- and medium-sized organisations, decisions about part-time higher education tended to be *ad hoc* and too fragmented for a clear policy to be apparent.

Future trends in employer demand

Several employers expected that the demand for part-time higher education would increase, although some said that this would substantially depend on individual decisions of students. Some perceived a large latent demand which might be tapped by better information and marketing. The employers of students on the Social

Care course all referred to the future of funding for public and voluntary sectors as a determinant of future support.

However, some employers, and some college and university staff, perceived a decline in employers' support for part-time courses. Employers were becoming more selective, focusing more narrowly on courses of direct relevance to the company. The balance in support between employer and student was shifting. Employers were more likely to demand a *quid pro quo* from the employee. For example, students might be required to demonstrate their own commitment by studying for the first year at their own expense and/or in their own time before an employer began to contribute. Instead of employers offering full day-release, they might offer an afternoon on the condition that the student matched it with an evening from his or her 'own' time. In other cases students might be expected to study in their own time in return for employer support for fees. The shipbuilding yard exemplified this trend. Formerly it had granted day-release but now it paid fees while expecting students to study in their own time. The college had scheduled the course for Friday afternoons when the yard was closed.

Aspects of provision which influence employer demand

We asked about aspects of provision which might influence or encourage demand. The responses varied. We interviewed two employers of Graphic Design students. One, a specialist unit within a large organisation, would have welcomed the opportunity to select individual HN units and omit those such as Communications, which he considered less relevant. The other needed widely-skilled employees and valued breadth – a very small enterprise, it looked to the college to define the field and did not feel confident to select from this field. Most employers welcomed the flexibility of colleges and their willingness to timetable courses to suit employers' needs. Flexibility in the time required to cover a course was not always welcomed; it could indicate poor organisation and day-release entitlements might not be extended beyond the allotted period. For some small enterprises, and for employers in the care sector, fees were an important factor. For others, they were a minor consideration. One large employer pointed out that college fees were far below those prevailing in the private sector and the main cost to the organisation was in terms of students' time, not fees. This employer would have been willing to pay higher fees for Accounting courses if they were scheduled to match the uneven flow of work, which generated one very busy week each month when students often had to miss classes. However, he recognised that this would probably not be cost-effective for the college because the monthly cycle differed across companies and other companies might not be able to pay higher fees. This comment may reflect a tacit recognition of higher education as a public service which should not be expected to run on purely market lines.

The communication of employer interests

When we asked employers how provision might be improved to respond to demand, it was apparent that many of them had given little thought to this and had not attempted to communicate their views to colleges or universities. Many employers seemed relatively passive in their relations with institutions. There were several reasons for this:

- as discussed above, in a majority of cases individuals and not employers were the immediate 'customers', even if employers were supporting the costs of study

- employers did not always have a clear, articulated view of their needs – in some cases (such as the small design firm mentioned above) they looked to the college to define the field

- they often had insufficient information about courses to make customer pressure effective

- colleges found it difficult to establish effective and continuous communication with employers, especially in relatively fragmented sectors, although employers were appreciative of such attempts as were made

- employers (especially small employers) might feel powerless in their dealings with the college (one employer told us how he had complained about what he felt was a badly-run course but his complaint got nowhere)

- small companies had neither the time nor the resources to initiate what could turn out to be a protracted dialogue with the college

- in fields such as accountancy, professional associations had the main role in defining course requirements

- the context of provision mattered – of the two colleges studied, one had a local monopoly in a buoyant labour market and the other faced local competition in a region of high unemployment and was more often described as responsive by the employers we talked to.

The factors listed above all varied according to the size of the employer, the structure of the industry, the state of the labour market and the nature and organisation of the occupation concerned. We did not interview enough employers to analyse these dimensions of variation very systematically. We heard of cases in which employer interests were effectively articulated and colleges were able to respond, for example by providing customised courses. However, the circumstances in which this was possible (for example large employers in stable industries with weak professional organisation) appeared not to apply for most of the employers we met.

The college with the 'local monopoly in a buoyant labour market', mentioned above, had a policy of creating Employer Liaison Committees (ELCs) across its broad spectrum of courses. Members were typically invited from large- and medium-sized organisations which currently or historically funded a number of employees for part-time courses. The ELCs for the two courses we studied had only recently been established and we got the impression that they were still finding their way and not yet in a position to consolidate around substantive issues. The existence of ELCs stemmed from the college's mission-oriented desire to respond to employer needs, yet on the Accounting course much of the dialogue on course revision was conducted at national level by SCOTVEC and the professional bodies. Consequently, we suspect that ELCs had more influence on issues of timetabling and delivery than on course content.

We can illustrate the diversity of employer-institution relationships by comparing four individual cases. They cover employers of very different sizes, from different sectors of the economy:

Keith Smith is training and development manager for a large engineering firm which supports many HNC students at College A. They pay fees as a matter of course and give time off as well, although in many cases the students use their own time for the course. The firm's relationship with the college goes back decades, perhaps to the college's foundation. Contact between the two is very regular, both at the formal level, through the engineering academic liaison committee, and in daily dealings, which Keith describes as 'dealing with the college's supply of services'. In other words, the college is looked on as a supplier just like any other supplier, such as the caterer, and the relationship is now on a strictly business footing. Ironically, this has actually resulted in a rise in the prices charged to the company as the newly incorporated college takes on its business role and the effect of a new market-driven approach has been to change both the character of the courses and the basis on which they are costed and charged. Several of the college's staff are former employees of the firm. The company is not very interested in increasing its intake of graduates and gives priority to technician level training. In short, the relationship is long-standing, operates within a traditional industry, is strongly underpinned by both formal and personal relationships and has adapted to a new market context.

Naila is an employer whose student is at the same college, doing Social Care. She runs a private kindergarten and Caroline is her first member of staff to attend the college, at least to her knowledge. Naila has visited the college once and was invited to attend the end-of-course party with her student but beyond that has had little contact. She encouraged Caroline to start on the course, in order for her to change career from child care to social work, and allows her to leave work 45 minutes early to attend college. On the debit side, she sees the studies as consuming energies as well as time: 'you can see the fatigue the next day'. Naila helps out with case study and project material but doesn't know enough about the college or course to be able to do this as effectively as she might. Her overall attitude to the college is summed up as, 'They were really nice, but if I'd known more about the course and how I could support the candidate, it would have helped'. In short, Naila is a small employer, untypical in the supportive attitude to her staff gaining qualifications (especially since these will probably mean that the employee leaves) but typifying some of the problems a college has in building an effective relationship with employers in a growing service area.

David is also a small employer, running a design company with a staff of nine. He himself, with three other members of the production staff, had attended courses at the college many years previously and, two years ago, had attended a meeting of the validation committee for the course on graphic design. He felt that the college had kept abreast of developments and, in some ways, was even ahead. The firm has no links with other educational institutions. David himself has no input into course content and is not aware of employer interests making inputs into national curricula or design qualifications via sectoral bodies, but the contact with the college means that the firm as well as the student is learning. He is happy to leave the choice of units to the college. As a small employer he requires breadth, because a small firm has to be versatile.

Finally, a rather unusual form of employer relationship comes from university C, which supports its own employees on a range of courses, including its own part-time degrees. Staff are encouraged to do the university's own courses, which include HNCs and HNDs as well as degrees. Some go elsewhere but the intention is to increase the proportion taking the university's own courses. A balance is struck between 'needs', relating to the university's training policy, and individual 'wants'. Employees who are granted support get fees paid and time off, including for exams, but no travel or book costs. The university now takes a closer interest in course content. The place of employee development in conditions of service is under active discussion, notably the relationship between the acquiring of qualifications and promotion or incremental pay rises. Interestingly enough, there is a fairly straightforward internal market – full fees are paid on behalf of employees taking university courses, despite attempts made recently by the staff development office to negotiate discounts. The university aims both to be a model employer in respect of human resource development and to contribute to its own mission as a provider of flexible learning opportunities.

Discussion

Despite employer support for many courses, in a majority of cases the students themselves were the immediate customers and the balance was shifting further in their direction. The triangular relationship of providers, students and employers is changing. Individual students are acquiring a greater role or (to put it a different way) employers are more reluctant to play the role that had been attributed to them in the past. This raises the question of whether institutional and national policies alike exaggerate the current importance of employers in determining the level and structure of demand.

Recent policies have encouraged colleges and universities to respond more effectively to employer demand. Our research leads us to question the current emphasis on institutional responsiveness, at least as this notion is currently understood, and with respect to undergraduate level higher education. The student, not the employer, is the principal customer of part-time higher education. Employers may not have a clear view of their needs – even if they do, the views of different employers may not coincide – and they may fail to communicate them effectively to the college. Employers are often remarkably passive in their dealings with colleges. A focus on college responsiveness may detract from the important potential for college leadership, for example by helping to disseminate technology and ideas in a field and by promoting concepts of learning organisation, especially in more fragmented sectors with weak industrial or professional organisation.

Our point is not that the notion of responsiveness is irrelevant but rather that, as currently understood, it does not apply in all contexts. It requires individual employers to play a purposive and proactive role which many employers, in many circumstances, have difficulty in playing. For these other employers and circumstances, different models of college–employer relationships may be required.

Chapter 10

Concluding Discussion

In this concluding chapter we draw together some of the main issues arising from our study.

Demand and supply

Our analysis of the trends and issues in part-time higher education needs to be set in the context of the massive expansion which has taken place in higher education over the last decade. Student numbers have grown enormously in both further education colleges and HEIs, and in both full-time and part-time modes. The growth is set to continue in both sectors, with the government committed to raising learning aspirations generally and, specifically, to ensuring that 500,000 extra places are available from 1998–99 onwards.

Demand and supply interact, of course. The growing responsiveness and customer consciousness of higher education and further education make the supply of opportunities increasingly sensitive to actual or latent demands. Conversely, the provision of more places means that more people become interested in the possibility of studying and the articulation of their latent demand elicits further supply, though not necessarily smoothly so. However, this spiral is not fixed, in shape or direction. The relationship between the two can change, for example in the proportions of full-time or part-time places which constitute the supply and the direction may change in the sense that expansion may be halted or even reversed for the system as a whole or for different sectors, institutions or modes within it.

We noted in Chapter 1 the kinds of arguments which have been made in favour of part-time higher education. One effect of this value commitment is that the case for part-time provision is customarily given rather more articulation than the arguments against it or the explanation for why, in the UK context, it has been so marginal. We cannot claim to have covered a full range of attitudes (we did not, for example, sample staff members generally for views for and against part-time provision) but one lesson from this study is that the logic of part-time provision is far from pervasive in its grip. Chapter 4 confirmed that part-time provision constitutes a relatively low proportion of all higher education. The following chapter showed the factors which influence the thinking of institutional policy makers, including the general desire to expand supply, the pragmatic necessity of searching for ways of increasing resources for the institution and a variety of cultural attitudes towards part-time provision and its place in the institution's mission. We have indicated that these can change quite rapidly, especially in response to changes in government funding, and this makes the provision of part-time higher education quite unpredictable. Chapters 5–9 illustrated how provision may be valued by those involved, without being able to root itself firmly in the institution's heart.

These institutional factors help us to understand the dynamics of the interaction of supply and demand. They need, however, to be linked to wider factors, notably changes in student finance, and in the labour market generally. Attitudes to higher education qualifications are shaped, amongst other things, by the perceived rewards which accrue to them and their perceived costs, material and otherwise. Arguably, we are going through a time of high volatility as far as these are concerned.

First, there has for some time been great uncertainty about current and future student funding systems, with a number of options being floated. This uncertainty was not settled by the publication of the Dearing Report – far from it since the new Labour government rejected the Dearing recommendation on student fees on the day the report was published. The balance between grant and loan has been quite radically adjusted and the student market is one where there can be long lags, with several years elapsing between changes in support systems and linked changes in behaviour. Attributing causality will also be a problem – it will be hard to tell how far any changes in student demand are due to changes in the funding system and how far to other factors.

Second, there is uncertainty about the demand for part-time higher education from employers. On the one hand the widespread rhetoric about lifelong learning should result in increased commitment to education in general terms on the part of employers. But, on the other hand, employers' actual support for part-time higher education students, in the form of contributions to fees or time off work, is becoming less dependable and more conditional. Some may choose to buy in specific training rather than use colleges as suppliers or to direct their employees towards the growing mass of open and distance learning packages, or to become suppliers themselves. Employees may be correspondingly uncertain about the precise occupational returns to part-time study, even if they still expect them to be positive.

Third, our study has demonstrated the importance of personal development and of the more 'generic' skills, both for students themselves and for employment. But, often, such skills are recognised and appreciated by students only after they have started to study and play less role in shaping their initial demand. Moreover, we have an impression that such skills are not well recognised, supported or rewarded by existing labour-market arrangements and that employers are increasingly confining their support to courses whose specific relevance can be demonstrated. This further increases uncertainties about future demand.

All of this means that the future of part-time higher education is hard to predict – a typically cautious researchers' conclusion. However, that caution nevertheless allows a categorical statement of a quite specific kind for it is clear that in Scotland part-time provision has not yet put down deep roots throughout the higher education system. If we consider its development against the backcloth of the explosion of higher education over the last decade, what is significant is the way it has continued to occupy a marginal position. It has grown in absolute numbers, but shrunk as a proportion of total numbers, and it remains concentrated in further education colleges, post-1992 universities and the OU. As far as the traditional core of the higher education system is concerned, the present is still full-time.

One way of looking at the future is to permute growth, decline and stability against full-time and part-time provision. Both modes could grow, one could decline and the other grow, or one or other or both could remain stable. A third dimension is the sectoral one, with growth or decline in either mode occurring differentially across sectors. We cannot predict what will happen but we can say that there is likely to be great unevenness in the patterns of future development. This may be no bad thing. Indeed, there is a strong case for diversity within the system in relation to part-time provision, as in many other respects. But whatever the rhetoric – strong and loud at the moment – for yet more expansion of education and training, there is no certainty that this will translate into effective demand or effective supply. And whatever the rationale – which we believe to be powerful – for strengthening part-time provision as a component of the whole, there is equally no certainty that this will materialise, whatever the intrinsic merits of the case. The arguments will continue to have to be given prominence. More than that, they will have to be backed up by suitable carrots and sticks if they are to prevail.

There are at least two push factors which may increase demand for part-time provision. The first is the growth in part-time employment, now one of the best-known features of the occupational landscape. Whilst it is true that many full-time students take part-time jobs and that the growth of these jobs does not benefit part-time students only, it clearly makes part-time study more possible as people look for combinations of work and study. Second, as attention is increasingly focused on the effectiveness of learning, the productive interaction between education and work that part-time study offers can only assume greater prominence and win support from employers and students alike.

However, there is a third factor which is the 'joker in the pack' for the future of part-time provision. How much longer will the original administrative/financial distinction between full-time and part-time provision be maintained? In other words, when will the fee-paying discrimination in favour of full-timers finally crumble away? The Kennedy Report on widening participation in further education makes the case powerfully for equity of funding and the debate around the government's consultation paper on lifelong learning can only strengthen public awareness of the current inequity. If this bias was to be removed, how much would demand shift in favour of part-time study? The students in our study felt that time rather than fees were the main disincentive to study, but these were the students whom the present fee structure had not deterred from studying part-time. There may be very many others who would be attracted back to education if a different funding regime was in place. Finally, if funding changes led to a switch in the balance of demand, how far would the institutions be equipped to respond?

Quality, standards and attainment

We are in a period when discussion of standards is politically and philosophically contentious and the issue of quality is the source of much internal concern, not least in the impact which approaches to its assessment and assurance have had on academic and administrative workloads. This has brought to the surface concerns about comparability across subjects and institutions (and across continents, with the franchising of degrees and the marketing of distance learning courses). Suggestions that there might be diversity in the standards of part-time provision are, therefore, potentially hazardous.

As with supply and demand, there is an inherent interaction between the nature of the student body and the question of quality. There are two aspects here which are central to the question of standards. First, our study has confirmed a general difference between full-time and part-time students which is broadly equivalent to the distinction between young and mature. Whilst there are many mature full-timers, there are relatively few young part-timers. Part-timers, therefore, generally exhibit most of the advantages and disadvantages of maturity when it comes to studying. Our study shows the former to outweigh the latter very considerably, at least in the eyes of the staff we talked to. Part-timers are more motivated, bring more experience to bear, teach each other more and absorb less unproductive energy on the part of the teacher. They may also be less sure of themselves academically, have less time to explore and develop their ideas and skills and be less able to build a culture of studenthood.

The second aspect is more specific. It derives from the assumption that learning which allows and draws on interaction with other aspects of life is likely to be more effective than that which does not. This is, of course, a generalisation and we acknowledge that there are many courses and subjects where interaction with the outside world is of no advantage and may even impede the in-depth development of thought. A job is the most obvious arena for such interaction, which partly explains why part-time provision is more prominent in subjects which have a direct link to defined occupations – as with several of our case study courses. Doing the accounts is likely to help those studying accountancy, just as delivering nursing care is likely to help those studying health. However, the wider contexts of social life offer similar opportunities for more general subjects.

Intrinsically, therefore, the interaction afforded by part-time study offers advantages. Against this must be set the time pressures which often exist on part-time students. This is not a necessary function of part-time study. For example, the students who were on traditional forms of day-release had no particular conflict, any more than being in a job imposed on them. Coming to college for the day was like going to work, except possibly more relaxed (this also reflects the fact that those studying in this mode were generally younger and without family responsibilities). But the vast majority – over 80 per cent – of our students were working full-time and there was, therefore, a constant claim on their time and energies. This is why it was common to find them satisficing rather than aiming for the highest grades.

We do not consider it possible to offer any research-based view on the narrow issue of whether standards are higher or lower, or, indeed, different in any salient respect between full-time and part-time. But it is possible to make the point that the value added is likely to be higher for part-time students, even where their attention is divided between the various parts of their lives. In other words, a relatively small amount of teaching can have a very substantial effect. Enrolment at an institution changes a person's attitude, converts external experiences into potential sources of learning and converts that person also into a source of learning for others. All of this happens with full-timers but it is fair to argue that it happens more commonly, and to a greater extent, with part-timers. That said, part-time provision gives an added complexity to the issue of academic standards and the extent to which they can be defined on a singular scale. The diversity it implies adds another item to the quality agenda for the future.

Advantages and disadvantages

We have discussed the advantages and disadvantages of part-time higher education, as seen from different perspectives, in several places in this report, notably in Chapter 5 from the perspective of institutional policy makers and in Chapter 8 from the perspective of the students. Below we present a diagrammatic overview of the advantages and disadvantages of part-time higher education reported by our respondents.

	Advantages	*Disadvantages*
To the student		
	• Access – a chance to study without surrendering job and income	• Time required to study
		• Strains on family and social life
	• Career benefits	• Fees
	• Personal gains – self-confidence, sense of achievement	• Marginality in institution
		• Narrowness – no time to read outside subject, miss social experience of student life
	• Educational benefits – using work and other experience	
	• Having a stable financial and temporal framework to study within	
	• Social benefits – meeting other students	
To the institution		
	• Achieving mission – e.g. access	• Conflict with mission – e.g. Research
	• Means to expand	• High administrative costs
	• Strengthening links with employers and community	• Development and overhead costs
	• Efficient use of resources	• Quality issues
	• Broadening student composition	
To individual staff		
	• Satisfaction from teaching mature and motivated students	• Unsocial hours
		• Increased workload
	• Developing new teaching approaches	• More demanding students
	• Contact with employers and occupational practice	
To employers		
	• More skilled workforce	• Time off job
	• Rewarding loyalty	• Fees

The question 'What are the (dis)advantages of part-time higher education?' can have several reference points. The point of comparison might be with full-time study or with no study at all, or it might be interpreted in a non-comparative way. We do not try to separate these out. There is often a running together of different factors.

A strong and deceptively simple framework for analysing advantages and disadvantages can be constructed using the two dimensions of *time* and *money*. We concluded the section on demand with the prospect of the collapse of the discrimination in student funding between full-time and part-time students. Part-timers receive less of a public subsidy than full-timers, so one clear advantage of part-time study is to the state. In this sense, part-time participation allows the externalisation of costs, with the student assuming the burden in place of the public purse. This is undoubtedly the case and we have at least illustrated the types of stress which can follow from this. But on both time and money, the issue is not straightforward.

Both dimensions have quantitative and qualitative aspects. There are more or less simple calculations to be made about the amount of money spent on studying, directly or in income foregone, and, similarly, about the amount of money to be gained, though this is necessarily more speculative. Yet even with money there are qualitative aspects, for example in the relative significance of different costs and benefits according to the social or lifecycle location of the student, especially where it is the household rather than the individual income which is at stake.

Time is naturally more complex and we can only illustrate here the way in which this dimension can be applied. One of the more surprising discoveries was the way in which part-timers can enjoy the advantage of a strong time structure at several different levels. At the daily and weekly level, because most of them were working, and working full-time, the time structure was supplied by their job. But employment also gives many part-timers a sense of continuity, however precarious the job may be – and even where their study is not linked at all to the job. This is in contrast to the full-timers, who may be preoccupied with what the future will bring for them and whether they should bring the future forward by leaving their studies. In short, and as a generalisation, although full-timers necessarily have the edge on part-timers as far as duration and speed of study are concerned (though not by as much as might be supposed), the position is reversed when it comes to temporal perspective.

The diagram above summarises the advantages and disadvantages to the different parties concerned. There remains the question of the extent to which part-time education generates a win-win set of circumstances or whether it favours one party at the expense of others. We have already said that, in general, the state can expect to be a gainer, which prompts the query why there is not stronger official support for part-time provision. For the other parties, the answer may well depend on the form of part-time provision. Thus employers are shifting away from day-release, primarily because of a clearer appreciation of the relatively high staff costs compared with the payment of fees for study done in the employee's own time. This constitutes a partial transfer of costs from employer to employee, but the deal may still be to the advantage of both. We have provided the occasional insight into consequences for family life. This is an area where further in-depth investigation would be particularly helpful.

The complexity of assessing advantages and disadvantages can be gauged if we point out that at least the following need to be taken into account in any comprehensive calculation: the criteria – implicit and explicit, material and non-material – used by the participants; the range of people regarded as having an interest (the effects on families, as we have just observed, are often ignored); the extent to which their perceptions are based on fact or supposition; and the extent to which they are liable to change, both during the study and after it has concluded. Finally, we must reiterate that 'part-time' covers a range of types of provision, which may generate different sets of advantage and disadvantage and the balance between them.

Having said all that, and bearing in mind the reservations made at the beginning of this chapter, we are happy to conclude by saying that we have no doubt that the advantages outweigh the disadvantages and that we are confident that the more attention is focused on them, and the more they are compared with full-time education, the stronger will be the case for enhanced part-time provision.

References

Anderson, C. (1960) *Grants to Students: Report of the Committee Appointed by the Minister of Education and the Secretary of State for Scotland in June 1958. Ministry of Education, SED.* London: HMSO

Ball, Sir C. (1990) *More Means Different.*, London: RSA.

Berg, L. and Kyvik, S. (1992) 'Part-time Studying at Norwegian Universities'. *Higher Education, 24,* 213–223.

Blackstone, T. (1991) 'Access, quality and governance: One institution's struggle for progess.' in T. Schuller (ed) *The Future of Higher Education.* Buckingham: SRHE and Open University Press.

Blackstone, T. and Williams, G. (1983) *Response to Adversity: Higher Education in a Harsh Climate.* Guildford: SRHE.

Blaxter, L. and Tight, M. (1993) 'Audience for part-time degree study'. *Research Papers in Education, 8,* 3, 369–387.

Blaxter, L. and Tight, M. (1994) 'Juggling with Time: How Adults Manage their Time for Lifelong Education'. *Studies in the Education of Adults, 26*(2) 162–179.

Bourner, T., Hamed, M., Barnett, R. and Reynolds, A. (1991) *Part-Time Students and their Experience of Higher Education.* Buckingham: SRHE and Open University Press.

Brannen, J., Moss P., Owen, C. and Wale, C. (1997) *Mothers, Fathers and Employment: Parents and the Labour Market in Britain 1984–94.* London: Department for Education and Employment.

Collfield, F. (ed) (1977) *A National Strategy for Lifelong Learning,* Newcastle: University of Newcastle.

Dearing, Sir Ron (1997) *Higher Education in a Learning Society: Report of the National Committee of Inquiry into Higher Education (Dearing Report).* London: HMSO.

Department for Education and Employment (1998a) *The Learning Age: A New Renaissance for a New Britain.* London: HMSO.

Department for Education and Employment (1998b) *Higher Education for the Twenty-First Century: Government Response to the Dearing Report.* London: HMSO.

Department for Education and Employment (1998c) *Higher Education for the Twenty-First Century: Government Response to the Garrick Report.* London: HMSO.

Department for Education and Employment, Scottish Office and Welsh Office (1995) *Lifetime Learning: A Consultation Document.* (Foreword by Gillian Shepherd, Michael Forsyth, William Hague). London: HMSO.

Dex, S. and McCulloch, A. (1995) *Flexible Employment in Britain: A Statistical Analysis.* Manchester: Equal Opportunities Commission.

Dickens, L. (1995) 'UK Part-time employees and the Law – Recent and Potential Developments'. *Gender, Work and Organisation, 2,*4, 207–15.

European Commission (1995) *Teaching and Learning: Towards the Learning Society.* Luxembourg: European Community.

Edwards, R. (1993) *Mature Women Students: Separating or Connecting Family and Education.* London: Taylor and Francis.

Fryer, R.H. (1997) *Learning For the Twenty-First Century.* First report of the National Advisory Group for Continuing Education and Lifelong Learning.

Fulton, O. (ed) (1989) *Access and Institutional Change*. Buckingham: SRHE and Open University Press.

Gallacher, J. and Sharp, N. (1995) *Working Together: Aspects of FE/HE Links in Scotland*. Working Paper, Glasgow Caledonian University.

Gallacher, J., Leahy, J., Sharp, N. and Young, A. (1989) *Part-Time Degree Provision in Scotland: Courses and Students 1987–88*. Glasgow College.

Gallie, D. and White, M. (1993) *Employee Commitment and the Skills Revolution*. London: Policy Studies Institute.

Garrick, Sir Ron (1997) *Higher Education in the Learning Society: Report of the Scottish Committee. National Committee of Inquiry into Higher Education (Garrick Report)*. London: HMSO.

Green, F., Ashton, D., Burchell, B., Davies, B. and Felstead, A. (1997) *An analysis of changing work skills in Britain*. Working Paper. University of Leeds.

Hewitt, P. (1996) The place of part-time work. In P. Meadows (ed) *Work Out – or Work In?* York: Joseph Rowntree Foundation.

Hoffman, R. and Inpeyre, J. (eds) (1998) *New Paths in Working Time Policy*. Brussels: European Trade Union Institute.

Keep, E. and Mayhew, K. (1995) The Economic Demand for Higher Education, and Investing in People – Two Aspects of Sustainable Development in British Higher Education. In F. Coffield (ed) *Higher Education in a Learning Society*. Durham: University of Durham.

Kennedy, H. (1997) *Learning Works: Report of the FEFC Committee on Widening Participation in Further Education (Kennedy Report)*. London: HMSO.

Lynn, P. (1996) *The 1994 Leavers: Scottish School Leavers Survey*. Edinburgh: Scottish Office Education and Industry Department.

MacFarlane, Alistair (1995) Future Patterns of Teaching and Learning. In T. Schuller (ed) *The Changing University?* Buckingham: SRHE and Open University.

McPherson, A. (1991) Widening the Access Argument. In T. Schuller (ed) *The Future of Higher Education*. Buckingham: SRHE and Open University Press.

National Commission on Education (1993) *Learning to Succeed*. London: Heinemann.

Nickell, S. (1997) 'Unemployment and Labor Market Rigidities: Europe versus North America'. *Journal of Economic Perspectives, 11*, 3, 55–74.

O'Reilly, J. and Fagan, C. (1998) *Part-Time Prospects: an International Comparison of Part-Time Work in Europe, North America and the Pacific Rim*. London: Routledge.

Paterson, L. (1997) 'Trends in participation in higher education in Scotland'. *Higher Education Quarterly, 51*, 29–48.

Raab, G. and Johnston, V. (1997) 'Higher Education in Scotland in the mid-1990s: A Statistical Summary Prepared for the National Enquiry into Higher Education in Scotland.' (unpublished paper) Edinburgh: Department of Mathematics, Napier University.

Raffe, D. (1994a) Flexibility in Vocational Education and Training: An Introduction. In W.J. Nijhof and J.N. Streumer (eds) *Flexibility in Training and Vocational Education*. Utrecht: Uitgeverijlemmabr.

Raffe, D., Brannen, K., Croxford, C. and Martin, C. (1997) *The case for 'home internationals' in comparative research: Comparing England, Scotland, Wales and Northern Ireland*. Working Paper, Centre for Educational Sociology, Edinburgh University.

Robbins, L. (1963) *Report of the Committee on Higher Education*. Cmnd 2154. London: HMSO

Robertson, D. (1994) *Choosing to Change: Extending Access, Choice and Mobility in Higher Education.* London: Higher Education Quality Council.

Robertson, D. and Hillman, J. (1997) *Widening participation in higher education for students from lower socio-economic groups and students with disabilities. Report 6 for the Dearing Committee.* London: HMSO.

Robertson, P. and Manacorda, M. (1997) *Qualifications and the labour market in Britain 1984-94: Skill biased change in the demand for labour or credentialism? Discussion Paper No 330.* Centre for Economic performance, London School of Economics.

Rubery, J. Smith, M. and Fagan, C. (1996) *Trends and Prospects for Women's Employment in the 1990s.* Brussels: European Commission.

Schuller, T. and Bostyn, A-M. (1992) *Learning: Education, Training and Information for the Third Age. Inquiry into the Third Age, Research Paper 3.* Dunfermline: Carnegie UK Trust.

Schuller, T. (ed) (1991a) *The Future of Higher Education.* Buckingham: SRHE and Open University Press.

Schuller, T. (1991b) 'Re-assessing the Future.' In T. Schuller (ed) *The Future of Higher Education.* Buckingham: SRHE and Open University Press.

Scott, P. (1995) *The Meanings of Mass Higher Education.* Buckingham: SHRE and Open University Press.

Scottish Office (1996) *Scottish Higher Education Statistics 1994–95, Statistical Bulletin Edn/32/1996/12.* Edinburgh: Government Statistical Service.

Scottish Office (1997) *Scottish Higher Education Statistics 1995–96. Statistical Bulletin: Education Series: Edn/J2/1997/12.* Edinburgh: Scottish Office.

Scottish Skills Forum (1996) *Report and Recommendations.* Glasgow: Scottish Enterprise.

Scottish Tertiary Education Advisory Council (STEAC) (1985) *Future Strategy for Higher Education in Scotland. Cmnd 9676.* Edinburgh: HMSO.

SCOTVEC (1995) *A Consultation Paper on Scotvec's Higher National Awards.* Glasgow: SCOTVEC.

Statistical Bulletin (1997) *Higher Education Institutions: Students and Staff 1995-6.* Edinburgh: Scottish Higher Education Funding Council.

Smith, D.M. and Saunders, M.R. (1991) *Other Routes: Part-time Higher Education Policy.* Buckingham: and Open University Press.

Tight, M. (1991) *Higher Education: A Part-Time Perspective.* Buckingham: SRHE and Open University Press.

Tremlett, N., Thomas, A., and Taylor, S. (1995) *Individual Commitment to Learning: Providers' Attitudes. Research Series no. 47.* Sheffield: Employment Department.

Watson, D. and Taylor, R. (1998) *Lifelong Learning and the University: A Post-Dearing Agenda.* Brighton: Falmer Press.

Williams, G. (1991) 'Finished and Unfinished Business.' In T. Schuller (ed) *The Future of Higher Education.* Buckingham: SRHE and Open University Press.

Williams, G. and Fry, H. (1994) *Longer-Term Prospects for British Higher Education. A Report to the Committee of Vice-Chancellors and Principals by the Centre for Higher Education Studies Institute of Education.* London: University of London.

Young, M. and Schuller, T. (1991) *Life After Work: The Arrival of the Ageless Society.* London: HarperCollins.

Subject Index

Author Index